Other U[image]
Commar[image]

MW01226574

Beginning/end of document	⌘-Home/⌘-End
Bullet (▲)	Option-8
Change style	⌘-Shift-S
Commands	⌘-Shift-Option-C
Show/hide ribbon	⌘-Option-R
Show/hide ruler	⌘-R
Double spacing	⌘-Shift-Y
Find	⌘-F
Go To	⌘-G
Hanging indent	⌘-Shift-T
Normal view	⌘-Option-N
Outline view	⌘-Option-O
Page Break	Shift-Enter
Page Layout view	⌘-Option-P
Print Preview	⌘-Option-I
Replace	⌘-H
Select columns	Option-drag mouse
Select entire document	Triple-click (in selection bar) *or* ⌘-A
Select paragraph	Triple-click (in text area)
Show/hide ¶	⌘-J
Subscript	⌘-Shift-–
Superscript	⌘-Shift-+

Books that Work Just Like Your Mac

As a Macintosh user, you enjoy unique advantages. You enjoy a dynamic user environment. You enjoy the successful integration of graphics, sound, and text. Above all, you enjoy a computer that's fun and easy to use.

When your computer gives you all this, why accept less in your computer books?

At SYBEX, we don't believe you should. That's why we've committed ourselves to publishing the highest quality computer books for Macintosh users. Externally, our books emulate the Mac "look and feel," with powerful, appealing illustrations and easy-to-read pages. Internally, our books stress "why" over "how," so you'll learn concepts, not sequences of steps. Philosophically, our books are designed to help you get work done, not to teach you about computers.

In short, our books are fun and easy to use—just like the Mac. We hope you find them just as enjoyable.

For a complete catalog of our publications:

SYBEX Inc.
2021 Challenger Drive, Alameda, CA 94501
Tel: (510) 523-8233/(800) 227-2346 Telex: 336311
Fax: (510) 523-2373

SYBEX is committed to using natural resources wisely to preserve and improve our environment. As a leader in the computer book publishing industry, we are aware that over 40% of America's solid waste is paper. This is why we have been printing the text of books like this one on recycled paper since 1982.

This year our use of recycled paper will result in the saving of more than 15,300 trees. We will lower air pollution effluents by 54,000 pounds, save 6,300,000 gallons of water, and reduce landfill by 2,700 cubic yards.

In choosing a SYBEX book you are not only making a choice for the best in skills and information, you are also choosing to enhance the quality of life for all of us.

WORD 5 FOR THE MAC
AT YOUR FINGERTIPS

▲

WORD 5 FOR THE MAC®
AT YOUR FINGERTIPS ▲

David Krassner

SYBEX ®

San Francisco ▲ Paris ▲ Düsseldorf ▲ Soest

Acquisitions Editor: Dianne King
Developmental Editor: Kenyon Brown
Editor: Janna Hecker Clark
Technical Editor: Celia Stevenson
Word Processors: Ann Dunn, Susan Trybull
Book Designer: Ingrid Owen
Chapter Art: Helen Bruno
Technical Art: Cuong Le
Screen Graphics: Arno Harris
Desktop Publishing Specialist: Dina F Quan
Proofreader/Production Assistant: Lisa Haden
Indexer: Anne Leach
Cover Designer: Ingalls + Associates
Cover Illustrator: Tom McKeith

Library of Congress Card Number: 92-81523
ISBN: 0-7821-1116-5

Manufactured in the United States of America
10 9 8 7 6 5 4 3 2 1

This book is dedicated to the memory of my own walking spirits—in particular, Walter and Joseph

ACKNOWLEDGMENTS

Many thanks to Ken Brown and Dianne King at SYBEX for giving me the opportunity to write this book.

It would not resemble a book at all, however, if it were not for the dedication, tireless effort, and unimpeachable expertise of the following persons at SYBEX: Janna Clark, editor; Celia Stevenson, technical editor; Ann Dunn and Susan Trybull, word processors; Cuong Le and Arno Harris, CAD; Dina Quan, typesetter; Helen Bruno, artist; and Lisa Haden, proofreader.

Heartfelt appreciation also goes to Christy Gersich and Microsoft, for supplying a copy of their wonderful new version of Word, as well as to Pamela McIver and Alki Software Corp. for generously providing the add-on software discussed in Part VII.

Thanks finally to Dean Lane-Smith, David Harvey, Will Baker, and Max Byrd, who taught me everything I know about writing.

Thank you all!

CONTENTS
AT A GLANCE

CONTENTS

PART II

PART III

PART IV

PART V

PART VI

PART VII

INTRODUCTION

Even as a longtime Microsoft Word user, I often found myself using just a fraction of this program's powerful features. This was only partly my fault, though: I never had a friendly guide to help me explore the capabilities of my favorite word processor.

A friendly, comprehensive guide is what this book is intended to be. *Word 5 for the Mac at Your Fingertips* is a function-oriented reference: I've arranged the book by function to help you learn *how* Word 5 works. Of course, the commands are here, too, so even when you have learned how to accomplish a task, you can still refer to *Word 5 for the Mac at Your Fingertips* time and time again as a quick reference. I can promise you, this book won't gather dust on the shelf!

As a special bonus, each section includes a *SnapGuide*. These are short essays filled with tips and advice on the functions being discussed, along with practical Word 5 and System 7 applications.

HOW THIS BOOK IS ORGANIZED ▲

Word 5 for the Mac at Your Fingertips is arranged in seven parts, each concerning itself with a distinct word processing function, as described below:

Part I outlines all the functions of Word 5, listing menu by menu all the commands at your disposal. The SnapGuide is an explanation of *Word 5's System-7 Savvy*—it describes how Word 5 takes advantage of System 7.

Part II discusses writing and editing documents. You will learn to start the program, to create a new document, to save your work, to open saved files, and to quit Word. You will also explore some of Word 5's unique document-composition tools, including the ribbon, ruler, and Word's three document views. This part's SnapGuide is on *Writing*.

Part III is all about formatting. One of the primary advantages of word processing over typing is the ability to enhance and size type (*fonts*). This part examines Word's singular abilities to work with characters, paragraphs, and sections. This part's SnapGuide is on *Professional Formatting*.

Part IV covers the many enhancements you can use to spiff up your Word documents. It discusses the new drawing facility, as well as headers and footers, footnotes, frames, tables, the indexing and TOC features, and voice annotations. This part's SnapGuide is on Word 5's *Object Linking Capabilities*.

In **Part V**, you'll learn the finer points of proofing your work. Discover how some features—the spell checker, grammar checker, thesaurus, and hyphenator—can improve the impact of your documents immeasurably. This part's SnapGuide is on *Proofing*.

Part VI discusses all the ins and outs of printing. Here, we will cover everything from margin settings to print merges. There is also a handy section on page numbering. This part's SnapGuide is on *Printing*.

For those who would like to customize the program, **Part VII** explains how you can change Word 5's default (factory) settings either temporarily or permanently. One of Word's most powerful features—customizable menus—is described in detail in this part. This part's SnapGuide, *Future Customization*, prepares you for new trends.

CONVENTIONS IN THIS BOOK ▲

To guide you quickly to important procedures, notes, related material, and keyboard shortcuts, this book uses repeating icons, which look like this:

PROCEDURE **NOTE** **SEE ALSO** **KEYBOARD SHORTCUT**

When related material is in a different part, the part number will be included with the name of the section.

xxi

The shorthand *Menu* ➤ *Command* will be used to indicate menu commands. For instance, if I ask you to "choose File ➤ Save," I mean "choose the Save command from the File menu."

You may notice that on your screen many command names are followed by an ellipsis (...), which indicates that the command leads to a dialog box. In this book I've omitted the ellipses, though, to avoid confusion.

Happy reading!

PART

EXPLORING
THE WORD 5 INTERFACE

———

The main reason I like Microsoft Word is that it often seems to intuit what I want to do. The program's seeming prescience is the result of a well-crafted interface. In this part, we'll explore Word 5's new interface, covering its application window and menus in depth. The *Snap-Guide* to *Part I* discusses the ways Word 5 takes advantage of System 7.

THE WORD 5 APPLICATION WINDOW

▲

———

When you start Word, the first thing you see is a new *document window*, as shown in Figure I.1. You can start typing immediately, using Word's default settings (creating a document is discussed in *Part II*). Let's take a moment now, though, to examine the elements that make up the application window.

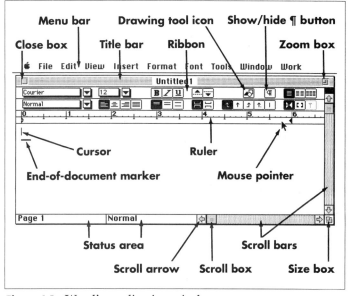

Figure I.1: Word's application window

▲ You access Word's menus from the *menu bar* at the top of the screen.

▲ The *title bar* shows the name of the document you are working on. The active window's title bar has gray stripes, while an inactive window's title bar is white.

▲ On the left edge of the title bar is the *close box.* Click this to close the active window.

▲ On the right edge of the title bar is the *zoom box.* Click once to shrink the document window; click again to return the window to its regular size.

▲ Just below the title bar is the *ribbon*. You can use the ribbon as a shortcut to apply several standard character formats and to change the font. Also, clicking on the drawing tool icon

brings up the drawing window and clicking on the show/hide ¶ button

displays or hides nonprinting characters (such as paragraph marks, tab marks, and space markers).

▲ Beneath the ribbon is the *ruler*. You can use the ruler to apply paragraph formats and alignments, change margins, apply styles, adjust tabs, or change the space between lines (the *leading*).

▲ The mouse pointer changes shape, depending on where it is. It is an arrow when hovering over a hot spot (such as a button or scroll bar) and an I-beam when you move it into the text window.

▲ The flashing bar is called the *insertion point* or *cursor*. Whatever you type or insert will appear at the cursor's position.

▲ The *end-of-document marker* tells you where the active document ends.

▲ The *status area* provides many different kinds of information (including font, style, page number, or section number), depending upon what you are doing.

▲ Click in the *scroll bars* to scroll vertically or horizontally through your document a screenful at a time. Clicking and dragging the *scroll boxes* does the same thing, although you can move much farther. To move in smaller increments (i.e., line by line) click the *scroll arrows*.

▲ Click and drag the *size box* to resize the document window.

SEE ALSO

Word 5's Menus

Part II, The New Ribbon and Improved Ruler

Part III: Formatting for Great Results

Part IV, You as the Artist

DIALOG BOXES

Many of the functions you perform in Word bring up *dialog boxes*. When Word shows a dialog box, it is effectively asking you how you would like your commands carried out. As you'll see, Word offers you several ways of doing almost everything. A typical dialog box (in this case, the Document dialog box) is shown in Figure I.2.

Let's look more closely at these dialog box elements.

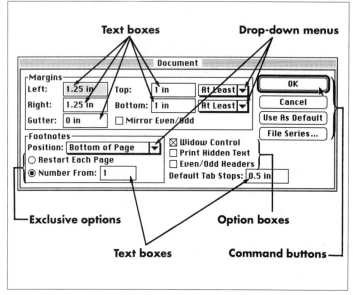

Figure I.2: A typical Word dialog box

▲ You can type specific settings in *text boxes.*

▲ If you click on a *drop-down menu,* you will reveal additional options.

▲ You choose *command buttons* to execute commands. Most dialog boxes have at least OK and Cancel, and many have an Apply button, which lets you see the effect of your settings before

INTERFACE

making them final. To select the command button surrounded by the heavy border

▲ press Return. Some buttons lead to other dialog boxes; these are distinguished by an ellipsis (…).

▲ The difference between *exclusive options* and *option boxes* is that you must choose one and only one option from an exclusive group, while you can select any or all options from a group of option boxes. Exclusive options use radio buttons; option boxes use check boxes.

WORD 5's MENUS

This book is structured to be function oriented—that is, to reflect the way people create documents. The menus in Word are also arranged with utility in mind, as indicated by their names. The best way to observe the value of this grouping is to examine each menu in detail.

 PROCEDURE

To select a menu command, click the name of the menu in the menu bar and slide the mouse pointer down to the command you want. Release the mouse button, and the command will flash.

NOTE

▲ If a menu command is dimmed, it is not available.

▲ Many commands have *keyboard shortcuts.* These are keys you can press to choose the command. If a command has a shortcut, it will be listed in the menu. In the sections below, shortcuts are shown in parentheses. Also, you can add shortcuts to any command (see *Part VII, Taking Command*).

The File Menu

The *File menu* contains the commands associated with manipulating files on disk.

▲ *New* (⌘-N) starts a new, untitled document.

▲ *Open* (⌘-O) opens a document.

▲ *Close* (⌘-W) closes the active document.

▲ *Save* (⌘-S) records on disk any changes you have made to the active document. If you are saving a document for the first time, this is the same as the Save As command.

▲ *Save As* records the active document under a different name.

▲ *Find File*, a new feature in Word 5, brings up a powerful file-retrieval utility. Many file-handling commands (File ➤ Open, Insert ➤ File, etc.) furnish a button to access this utility.

INTERFACE

▲ *Summary Info,* also new to Word 5, brings up a dialog box where you can provide information about your document. The Find File utility searches for files using this information.

▲ *Print Preview* (⌘-Option-I) displays your document in an uneditable preview mode. Use this before printing to determine whether all your page elements are in their correct positions.

▲ *Page Setup* brings up the dialog box where you record your page specifications (including size, orientation, and other options).

▲ *Print* (⌘-P) prints the active document.

▲ *Print Merge* initiates the Word function that generates mass mailings.

▲ *Quit* (⌘-Q) shuts down Word and all its documents. If you have any documents with unsaved changes, you will be given a chance to record them to disk.

 SEE ALSO

Part II: Learning the Basics

Part VI: Printing Your Documents

The Edit Menu

The commands on the *Edit menu* include many revising tools, as well as some of Word 5's more esoteric file-linking facilities.

▲ *Undo* (⌘-Z) is a lifesaving tool. You can undo most editing and many functions. The name of this command changes, depending on what you've just done. Be aware that this undoes only your most recent command; choosing Undo again undoes the undo.

▲ *Repeat* (⌘-Y) performs different functions depending upon the circumstances. It essentially repeats whatever typing, deleting, or pasting you've done most recently. Be prepared to experiment with Repeat.

▲ *Cut* (⌘-X) removes any highlighted material from the document and places it in the Clipboard.

▲ *Copy* (⌘-C) makes a copy of any highlighted material in the document and places it in the Clipboard.

▲ *Paste* (⌘-V) inserts a copy of whatever is in the Clipboard into your document at the cursor.

▲ *Paste Special* allows you to specify what format pasted material should adopt.

▲ *Clear* is a table command; it removes any data from the highlighted cells without putting it in the Clipboard.

INTERFACE

▲ *Select All* (⌘-A) selects all material in the active document.

▲ *Find* (⌘-F) activates Word's revamped text locator.

▲ *Replace* (⌘-H) activates Word's improved text-replacing utility.

▲ *Go To* (⌘-G) takes you to a specific page of a document.

▲ *Glossary* (⌘-K) brings up the Glossary dialog box (a list of automatic text features).

▲ *Create Publisher* places any highlighted material in a special file called an *edition*. The edition file can in turn be *subscribed* to by other documents (see Subscribe To, below). Any changes made to the edition file will be reflected in subscriber documents.

▲ *Subscribe To* brings up the Subscribe dialog box, where you can subscribe to edition files.

▲ *Options* (variously called *Link Options, Publisher Options,* and *Subscriber Options*) controls the behavior of specific links, published editions, and subscribers.

▲ *Edit Object* opens whatever program created the object. An object must be selected to use this command.

SEE ALSO

Part II: Learning the Basics

Part III, Using the Glossary

Part IV, Setting Up Tables

Part IV, SnapGuide to Object Linking in Word 5

The View Menu

The commands on the *View menu* offer you not only different ways to look at your documents, but also choices about which Word tools appear in the document window.

▲ *Normal* (⌘-Option-N) shows your document in the standard editing view. (This is the default.)

▲ *Outline* (⌘-Option-O) shows your document in a lean, headings-only view that makes the structure apparent.

▲ *Page Layout* (⌘-Option-P) shows your document as it will print, with all page elements in place. This view is WYSIWYG (*what you see is what you get*).

▲ *Ribbon* (⌘-Option-R) and *Ruler* (⌘-R) show or hide the ribbon and ruler (both discussed above in the section *The Word 5 Application Window*).

▲ *Print Merge Helper* is a powerful new Word 5 feature that automates the construction of the main and data documents used in print merges.

▲ *Show/hide ¶* (⌘-J) shows or hides nonprinting characters, such as paragraph marks, hyphens, and space markers.

▲ *Header* opens a header window (in Normal view), where you can specify information that is to print at the top of every page.

▲ *Footer* opens a footer window (in Normal view), where you can specify information that is to print at the bottom of every page.

▲ *Footnotes* (⌘-Shift-Option-S) splits your document window, opening a footnote pane at the bottom.

▲ *Voice Annotations* shows a list of all voice annotations in the document. You can listen to them, too.

 SEE ALSO

Part II: Learning the Basics

Part IV: Enhancing Your Work with Word 5's Special Features

Part VI: Printing Your Documents

The Insert Menu

You can insert just about anything into a document via the *Insert menu*. You will find yourself visiting the Insert menu when you want to add a special feature to enhance a document.

▲ *Page Break* (Shift-Enter) ends the current page and begins a new one.

▲ *Section Break* (⌘-Enter) ends the current section and begins a new one.

▲ *Table* inserts a table at the cursor after allowing you to specify the number of rows and columns and the width of columns.

▲ *Footnote* (⌘-E) inserts a footnote marker and opens a footnote pane, where you can type the text of the footnote.

▲ *Voice Annotation* activates Word 5's new feature that lets you add recorded comments to documents.

▲ *Date* places a glossary *entry* at the cursor, showing the current date.

▲ *Symbol* opens a chart of special symbols (such as accented characters, ß, £, ™, etc.). Click on a symbol to insert it at the cursor.

▲ *Index Entry* inserts an index field, indicating to Word that whatever is typed there should be included when Word compiles an index.

▲ *Index* compiles an index, using those entries coded as index entries.

▲ *TOC Entry* inserts a table of contents (TOC) field, indicating to Word that whatever is typed there should be included when word compiles a TOC.

▲ *Table of Contents* compiles a TOC, using those entries coded as TOC entries.

▲ *Frame* inserts a movable container in which you can place text, pictures, or other objects. This is a wonderful new Word 5 command that effectively bridges the gap between word processors and low-end desktop publishers. Since a frame and its contents act as a unit, wherever you move a frame, its contents will follow.

▲ *File* inserts an entire file from disk at the cursor.

▲ *Picture* opens Word's new drawing tool. Whatever you create in the drawing window will be placed in your document at the cursor position.

▲ *Object* allows you to insert nontext material into a document (such as pictures, equations, and Excel spreadsheets and charts).

 SEE ALSO

Part III: Formatting for Great Results

Part IV: Enhancing Your Work with Word 5's Special Features

The Format Menu

The commands under the *Format menu* all handle various aspects of character, paragraph, and document formatting.

▲ *Character* (⌘-D), *Paragraph* (⌘-M), *Section*, and *Document* each open dialog boxes with options specific to their functions.

▲ *Border* doesn't do anything you couldn't do with earlier versions of Word, but it does make adding a border to paragraphs, frames, and so on much easier. Many format-related commands (Format ➤ Character, Format ➤ Table Layout, etc.) furnish a button to access this command.

▲ *Table Cells* and *Table Layout* are table-specific commands that govern the appearance and proportions of tables.

▲ *Frame* manages the size and placement of frames.

▲ *Style* (⌘-T) opens the Style dialog box, where you can modify existing styles or create new ones.

▲ *Revert To Style* (⌘-Shift-Spacebar) changes all highlighted text back to the default style for the paragraph (that is, undoes any additional formatting or font changes you've made).

▲ *Change Case* brings up a dialog box that offers you five different ways to upper- and lowercase the highlighted text.

▲ *Plain Text* (⌘-Shift-Z) removes any character formatting from the highlighted text.

▲ *Bold* (⌘-B), *Italic* (⌘-I), and *Underline* (⌘-U) apply character formatting to the highlighted text.

SEE ALSO

Part III: Formatting for Great Results

Part IV, Setting Up Tables

The Font Menu

The *Font menu* allows you refined control over the fonts in your document.

▲ To increase or decrease the *size* of your font, high-light the text you want to change and choose the desired size from the Font menu.

▲ *Up* (⌘-]) increases the font size by 1 pt (point). The change appears in the status area.

▲ *Down* (⌘-[) decreases the font size by 1 pt. Again, the change appears in the status area.

▲ *Other* opens the Character dialog box, where you can specify additional text enhancements.

▲ *Default Font* opens the Preferences dialog box (nor-mally reached by choosing Tools ➤ Preferences) and selects the Default Font category. You can then change the default font for the document if you wish.

▲ To change the *font* you are using, highlight the text you want to modify and choose the desired font from the Font menu.

 SEE ALSO

Part III: Formatting for Great Results

Part VII: Customizing Word 5

The Tools Menu

Something of a catchall, the *Tools menu* includes the proofing tools (the grammar and spell checkers), several database and math features, and the all-powerful Preferences command.

▲ *Spelling* (⌘-L) activates the spelling facility. You should *always* have Word check your spelling, even if you intend to check it manually. The spell checker in Word 5 is far better than its predecessors and has an almost uncanny ability to discern what you were trying to say.

▲ *Grammar* (⌘-Shift-G) starts Word 5's new grammar checker. This feature checks your documents for various rules of word usage, punctuation, and even spelling. At present, though, the grammar checker is infuriatingly slow.

▲ *Thesaurus* is one of my favorite new Word 5 commands. This fast, intuitive feature suggests synonyms to vary your diction and spice up your prose.

▲ *Hyphenation* launches the automatic hyphenation feature. This can make your paragraphs a lot more aesthetically pleasing.

▲ *Word Count* brings up an information box telling you how many characters, words, lines, and paragraphs you have in your document. This can be helpful if you have a word limit.

▲ *Renumber* either adds numbers to lines or paragraphs, or changes numbered lines and paragraphs
to make the numbers sequential. This command is
flexible, allowing you to determine the starting number, the format, etc.

▲ *Sort* rearranges all selected paragraphs, placing
them in ascending alphanumeric order.

▲ *Calculate* (⌘-=) finds the sum of any highlighted
numbers in your document. You can perform
other mathematical functions as well.

▲ *Repaginate Now* instructs Word to determine where
all your pages will break.

▲ *Preferences* opens the Preferences dialog box. Here
you can customize Word to look and function in a
way that best suits your work habits.

▲ *Commands* (⌘-Shift-Option-C) opens the Word
Commands dialog box. You can add or remove
commands from menus and specify keyboard
shortcuts here.

 SEE ALSO

*Part IV: Enhancing Your Work with Word 5's Special
Features*

Part V: Proofing: The Finishing Touches

Part VII: Customizing Word 5

The Window Menu

The *Window menu* greatly simplifies working with multiple documents.

▲ *Help* summons Word's vast help utility.

▲ *Show Clipboard* shows the Clipboard window so you can see what's there.

▲ *New Window* opens an additional window for the active document. It is named with the document's name plus *:2*, *:3*, and so on. You might use this if you wanted to see the same document in several different views. Note that all windows opened with this command are looking at the same document; changes in one window will be reflected in the others.

▲ Finally, there will be a *list* of all documents you have open. To switch from one document to another, simply choose the desired one's name from the Window menu.

The Work Menu

You will not see the *Work menu* when you first start Word. It is added to the menu bar only if you instruct Word to place it there, which you do by adding certain menu commands. The kinds of items you place on the Work menu are glossary entries, styles, commands, and even documents. See *Part III, Using the Glossary* for more details.

SNAPGUIDE TO WORD 5's SYSTEM-7 SAVVY ▲

System 7's powerful document-linking capabilities, intuitive file-manipulation functions, and many nifty features far outweigh its shortcomings. Word 5 is *System-7 Savvy*, that is, it takes full advantage of System 7's new functionality. In this SnapGuide, I'll introduce those features of Word 5 that best illustrate how powerful it can be when running under System 7.

Multitasking

In previous system versions, you could choose to *multitask* (run several applications simultaneously) or to run in single-application mode. System 7, however, multitasks automatically. But beware: Multitasking is addictive. Once you've enjoyed the convenience and versatility of jumping between open applications (including the Finder), you'll probably never want to go back to single-application mode.

Word 5 doesn't run any worse in single-application mode than under MultiFinder, but you'll find probably feel constrained all the same.

For instance, under System 7, you can switch over to other programs—such as Excel or 4th Dimension—to get figures or data and then return to Word with a mouse-click. In single-application mode, the same cross-referencing would entail quitting Word, returning to the

Finder, starting Excel or 4D from scratch, finding the information, *closing* Excel or 4D, *returning* to the Finder again, and *restarting* Word. Clearly, you waste a lot of valuable time.

In addition to its convenience, there are certain features of Word 5 that simply don't work if you're not operating under System 7. These include document linking.

Sharing Information

To use the *publish and subscribe, object linking,* or *embedding* features of Word 5, you must be running under System 7. These file-linking commands do not work under earlier system versions.

Which option you use to share information will depend upon how dynamic that information is. Generally speaking, publish and subscribe is used when the information is to be changed often, particularly over a network. Object linking works well when your information is subject to frequent changes, but is confined to one Mac. If your information is on one computer and is seldom changed, embedding is the best choice.

 NOTE

You can *embed* objects into Word 5 documents whether you are running System 7 or not. In single-application mode, though, you are limited to objects you can create in or import into Word. These include drawings made with the drawing facility, equations made with Equation Editor, and some disk files. There are no dynamic links in this case.

SEE ALSO

Part IV, SnapGuide to Object Linking in Word 5

TrueType Fonts

TrueType fonts are the evolutionary successors to *bitmap* fonts. Bitmaps come in specific sizes; if you shrink or enlarge them, they look lousy. TrueType fonts, though, are *scalable.* You can change them to almost any size and they will be perfectly smooth and well proportioned. This is because TrueType fonts are stored as a series of connected curves and lines, the proportions and angles of which are all carefully defined.

You can use TrueTypes only under System 7. See *Part III, Using Fonts Effectively,* for more information.

Aliases and the Apple Menu

One of System 7's cleverest new gadgets is the *alias.* An alias is a pointer file that contains location information for the original file. It allows you to launch an application program by a different name. You can make aliases for any document or application and then move them anywhere you like. This means you can leave files buried several folders deep—which you may want to do for organizational reasons—but still access them without a lot of hunting.

One very effective use of aliases is to place them in the Apple Menu Items folder so they appear on the Apple menu. Then, whenever you need a file or application, you simply choose its alias. See *Part II, Using an Alias* for further details.

Balloon Support

A double-edged sword, Balloon Help can be a learning tool for users new to Word. When Balloon Help is enabled, comic-strip balloons pop up with descriptions of the commands as you move the mouse pointer around the screen. This can be very annoying, though, because normal use of Word makes balloons explode all over the place. See *Part II, Balloon Help.*

PART

II

LEARNING
THE BASICS

———

Even with the recent boom in desktop-publishing features, some of the greatest advantages of word processing over typing remain the ease and speed with which you can revise your work. In this part, we'll explore how to start Word, create a document from scratch, save it, and then recall it for editing. In the process, you'll learn how to print, find lost files, and get help when you need it.

STARTING WORD   ▲
———

There are four ways to start Word from the Finder:

- ▲ Open the program itself
- ▲ Open a document created in Word or a Word-support file (such as a glossary)
- ▲ Open an *alias* of the program or document
- ▲ Drag a non-Word document onto the Word program icon

The first two options are fairly straightforward. To open Word, a Word document, or a Word-support file, you simply double-click on an icon in the Finder.

Word 5.0   Glossary   Buddenbrooks

Word-support files include glossaries, dictionaries, and settings files. The second two options are a bit trickier. Let's look at them in a little more detail.

KEYBOARD SHORTCUT

Instead of double-clicking to open a file, you can highlight its icon and press ⌘-O.

Using an Alias

Aliases, though more work to set up, ultimately provide an easier way to start Word than opening a document or support file. New to System 7, aliases can be made for any document or application and then moved anywhere you like. The advantage of aliases is that you can leave original files buried several folders deep, as you may wish to do for organizational reasons, but still access them through aliases without a lot of hunting.

One very effective use of aliases is on the Apple menu. First, you place an alias in the Apple Menu Items folder. Then, whenever you need a file or application, you simply choose its alias. Moving an alias of an application is better than moving the application itself, because an application that has been relocated often has trouble finding its support files.

 PROCEDURE

To add a Word 5 alias to your Apple menu, follow these steps:

1. Go to the Finder to locate and highlight the Word 5 program icon.

2. Choose File ➤ Make Alias.

3. Drag the Word 5 *alias* icon (its name will be italicized and the word *alias* will be appended) into the Apple Menu Items folder.

The alias will appear on the Apple menu. Select it anytime you want to start Word (even while you are running another program under System 7).

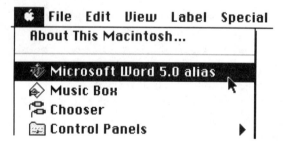

Opening Non-Word Documents

A nifty new trick Word 5 can perform is opening documents created in many other programs. This is handy if, for instance, someone gives you a file written with an application you don't own. With previous versions of Word, if you didn't have the specific application, you were out of luck. But now you can take advantage of all Word 5's goodies, even if the files you're working with weren't written in Word 5.

 PROCEDURE

To open a non-Word document, simply drag the document onto the Word 5 program icon. If nothing happens, it means that Word cannot read the file's format).

 SEE ALSO

Opening a File from Disk

OPENING A NEW DOCUMENT ▲

If you were able to start up Word, you've already opened a new document without doing anything—an untitled file appears automatically when the program starts. Figure I.1

in *Part I* shows a new document window and identifies the standard elements of a Word window. Starting a new document after Word has been running for a while is almost as easy.

PROCEDURE

To open a new document, choose File ➤ New. A new document, named *Untitledx* (*x* is the number of new documents you've opened during your current session), will appear.

KEYBOARD SHORTCUT

⌘-**N** opens a new document.

COMPOSING YOUR DOCUMENT ▲

As you learn Word 5, you'll find yourself developing certain work habits. For instance, you might always set your margins and tabs before you begin work on a document. While these are good practices, one great advantage of Word is its flexibility. You can decide formatting issues either before or after you write your documents. While I prefer to make such decisions prior to writing, the *last* thing I want to do is regiment your work!

That said, the simple truth to composing in Word is that you just start typing.

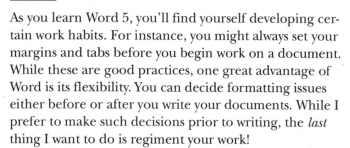

NOTE

If you've never used a word processor before, you may be surprised by some things Word does. For example, you'll notice that Word automatically *word-wraps* text when it reaches the right margin. Do *not* hit Return when you reach the ends of lines: this will muck things up if you want to revise your document. In fact, if you're used to typing, there are several other habits you should break in order to get the most out of Word:

▲ Do *not* use the Spacebar to make paragraph indents or to align things. (You will probably be using proportionally spaced fonts, which are impossible to align manually.) Use the Tab key instead.

▲ Do *not* use tabs in lists like this one where the first line extends beyond the left margin of the paragraph. Use *hanging indents* instead.

▲ Do *not* use tabs to arrange complex columns of information; use Word's Table feature instead. (For simple tasks, like phone lists, tabs are okay.)

▲ Don't repeatedly hit Return to force material onto a new page. Instead, use Word's Insert ➤ Page Break command (Shift-Enter).

PROCEDURE

To compose a document from scratch, simply begin typing at the keyboard. If you make a mistake, either hit the Delete key to back over it or highlight the mistake with the mouse and type in the correction. Notice that what you type replaces what you have highlighted.

MOVING AROUND ▲

You will almost always want to edit a new document as you go along. If so, you'll find yourself moving around a lot. The easiest way to do so is through judicious use of the mouse and the scroll bars.

 PROCEDURE

To move from one point to another, click in the scroll bar to find the desired place in the document. Then click in the text window to position the cursor or double-click to highlight the material you want to change.

 NOTE

You'll get different results, depending upon the number of times you click the mouse button:

Click...	*To*...
Once	Position the cursor
Twice	Select an entire word
Three times	Select an entire paragraph

SEE ALSO

Word's Three Views

Revising Your Work

Part III, Tabbing

Part III, Indenting

Part III, Moving Your Margins

BASICS

SAVING YOUR WORK ▲

I cannot overemphasize the importance of *saving your work frequently.* With Word, you can save a document to disk before you even compose it, which is not a bad idea.

 PROCEDURE

To save your work, choose File ➤ Save. If you are saving for the first time, you will get the dialog box shown in Figure II.1. Give the file a relevant name and click Save. If the file has already been saved and you select File ➤ Save, the copy on screen will replace the one on disk automatically, and you will not see a dialog box.

 KEYBOARD SHORTCUT

⌘-S is the shortcut for saving a document.

Figure II.1: The Save As dialog box

NOTE

If you do not wish to save the file to the current folder or disk, you can change them. To change the disk, click on the Desktop button and choose the correct disk. To change the folder, click on the folder icon above the folder box. A folder list will drop down, allowing you to select the folder you want.

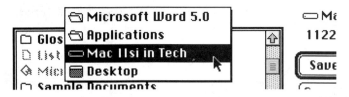

If you wish to save your file in a format other than Word 5, choose a format from the Save File as Type drop-down list. You have an extensive range of choices, including Word-Perfect and Word for Windows.

Stationery

One of the options in the Save File as Type list is Stationery, a new feature in Word 5. When you save a file as stationery, you are making it a *template*; that is, each time you open it, it will be exactly the same. If you make changes to a stationery file, you have to save them under a new file name. Stationery icons even look different from regular document icons.

Letterhead

The advantages of stationery files are more apparent when considered in terms of formats and repeated elements. Imagine stationery files on your computer as being similar to your personal writing stationery and you'll get the idea. For example, you could have a stationery file for your letterhead. Each time you wanted to send a business letter, you could call up the stationery document; then when you printed the letter, it would already be on letterhead. To further reduce your work, you could even save your signature block as part of the stationery.

 SEE ALSO

Part III: Formatting for Great Results

Part IV: Enhancing Your Work with Word 5's Special Features

Summary Info

The first time you save a document, you will be assailed by a wayward dialog box called Summary Info (shown in Figure II.2), and also new to Word 5. Any information you add to this box can be used by Word 5's new File ➤ Find File command. If you have a lot of files or work for an organization with lots of users, it is a good idea to take the time to fill in the Summary Info fields.

Summary Info	
Title:	1001 Things to Do with Peaches
Subject:	alternative uses for cling peache
Author:	David Krassner
Version:	draft
Keywords:	peach, cow, Wankle-rotary engi

OK
Cancel

Figure II.2: The Summary Info dialog box

If you prefer, you can defer this task to later. When you want to add information to or amend a Summary Info box, just choose File ➤ Summary Info.

SEE ALSO

Finding the Prodigal File

Automatic Saving

This feature may someday save you from anguish and grief. The concept is simple: have Word periodically remind you to save your work. And yet this is the first version of the software that has it. *Oi vey!*

 PROCEDURE

To have Word remind you to save your work, follow these steps:

1. Choose Tools ➤ Preferences.

2. In the Preferences dialog box, click on the Open And Save category.

3. Click on the Save Reminder Every *x* Minutes option, if there is no X in the check box.

 ⊠ **Save Reminder Every** 7 **Minutes**

4. Change the interval if you find the default either too frequent or infrequent.

5. Close the Preferences dialog box.

 NOTE

Word does not actually save files automatically. You are prompted by a little dialog box at the specified interval to save your file.

You can either postpone saving by clicking Cancel or click OK to save.

SEE ALSO

Part VII, Preferences

Automatic Backup

If you like to experiment with different versions of a document, the Make Backup option can help. This handy little option, when activated, will save the *previous* version of a document each time you save a revised version. The previous version is always called *Backup of ...* and the file name. The advantage to making backups is that, even if you mangle a file irreparably and then accidentally save it, you can still retrieve a "good" old version of it.

PROCEDURE

To activate automatic backup, choose File ➤ Save As and click on the Make Backup option. Then click OK.

You will then be asked "Replace existing *filename*?" Click on Replace.

 KEYBOARD SHORTCUT

Shift-F7 is the keyboard shortcut for the Save As command.

 SEE ALSO

Saving Your Work

Closing a Document

When you *close* a document, you are only removing it from RAM, not deleting it from disk.

 PROCEDURE

To close the active document, choose File ➤ Close or click the close box on the left edge of the title bar.

 KEYBOARD SHORTCUT

⌘-W is the shortcut for closing a document.

WORD'S THREE VIEWS ▲

Depending upon the situation, there are more and less practical ways to view your document. For example, when you are first writing a document, there is usually no need to see how the document will look when printed. When you are outlining a report, it is useful to be able to view selected levels of your outline. In mind of your varying needs, Microsoft kindly provides three different *views* for Word documents:

- ▲ Normal
- ▲ Outline
- ▲ Page Layout

There is a fourth "view," Page Preview, but it is really an uneditable, bird's-eye variation of Page Layout. We will explore it in *Part VI: Printing Your Documents*. For now, let's examine each of the views in detail, considering their advantages and disadvantages.

Normal

Normal view is the default view. You will usually use Normal view when you are writing documents. It is also adequate for most editing jobs. Figure II.3 shows a document (found in the Sample Folder provided with Word 5) in Normal view.

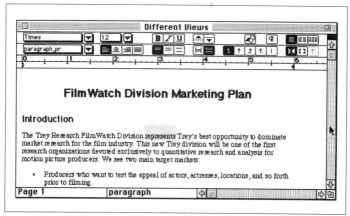

Figure II.3: A document in Normal view

There is a graphic in this document that is not visible in Normal view because it's in the header. But, as you can see, all the text and paragraph attributes are apparent.

 PROCEDURE

To activate Normal view, choose View ➤ Normal. This is the default view; when you start Word, you are in Normal view.

Advantages

The advantages of Normal view are:

▲ Text scrolling is swift

▲ All text is visible

▲ Editing is easy

▲ All paragraph formatting (e.g., line spacing) is evident

▲ You have access to the ruler

▲ All proofing and enhancement tools are available (e.g., spell checker, frames, footnotes)

Disadvantages

The disadvantages of Normal view are:

▲ The organization of the document is difficult to see

▲ Columns or other paragraph arrangements are not visible

▲ You can't see frames, graphics, headers and footers, or footnotes in place

▲ You can't see the actual layout of the page (e.g., margins, page edges, and page numbers)

 KEYBOARD SHORTCUT

⌘-**Option-N** is the shortcut for Normal view.

 **SEE ALSO**

Part IV: Enhancing Your Work with Word 5's Special Features

Part VI: Printing Your Documents

Outline

Outline view is similar to Normal view in some respects, but is intended for document organization, not composition. Figure II.4 shows a document in Outline view.

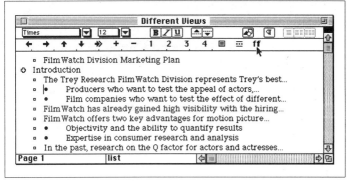

Figure II.4: A document in Outline view

Notice that you don't see any paragraph or text attributes. Also, many of the paragraphs end with an ellipsis (...), denoting more text below. Note the special outline tool bar near the top of the screen. Its buttons are described in detail on the inside back cover of this book.

PROCEDURE

To activate Outline view, choose View ➤ Outline.

Advantages

The advantages of Outline view are:

▲ Shows organization clearly

▲ You can designate the level of organization you wish to see

▲ Reorganization is quick, due to special tools

▲ Hierarchical distinctions (e.g., underscoring of highest head levels and indenting of lower levels) are automated

Just to give you a hint of how easy it is to reorganize documents in Outline view, let's transpose the first two bulleted items.

 PROCEDURE

To move a paragraph in Outline view, follow these steps:

1. Move the mouse pointer toward the left margin until it becomes a crosshair, then click once to select the paragraph.

⬦ Introduction
　▫ The Trey Research FilmWatch Division represents Trey's best...
　✛• Producers who want to test the appeal of actors,...
　▫ • Film companies who want to test the effect of different...
　▫ FilmWatch has already gained high visibility with the hiring...

2. Click and drag the paragraph until you see the dotted line where you want to move the paragraph.

⚙ Introduction
  ▫ The Trey Research FilmWatch Division represents Trey's best...
  ▪ • Producers who want to test the appeal of actors,...
↨ ▫ • Film companies who want to test the effect of different...
  ▫ FilmWatch has already gained high visibility with the hiring...

3. Release the mouse button, and the paragraph will fall neatly into its new position, text and all.

Disadvantages

The disadvantages of Outline view are:

▲ Scrolling can be *very* slow

▲ Editing can be cumbersome

▲ Not all material is visible by default (and showing material often defeats the purpose of using this view)

▲ You can't access the ruler; many proofing and en-hancement tools are unavailable (e.g., spell checker, frames, footnotes)

▲ Paragraph formatting is ambiguous

▲ You can't see columns or other paragraph arrangements

▲ You can't see frames, graphics, or other elements in place

▲ You can't see the actual layout of the page

KEYBOARD SHORTCUT

⌘ -**Option-O** is the shortcut for Outline view.

 **SEE ALSO**

Part VI: Printing Your Documents

Page Layout

Page Layout view is most beneficial when you are trying to determine how a document's pages should look when printed. Figure II.5 shows a document in Page Layout view.

Now you can see the graphic in the header, along with some rather complicated PostScript instructions. When this document is printed (the margins and page edges are now obvious), these instructions will print the word *Confidential* as a diagonal backscreen (a *watermark*) in huge type across every page.

 PROCEDURE

To activate Page Layout view, choose View ➤ Page Layout.

Figure II.5: A document in Page Layout view

Advantages

The advantages of Page Layout view are:

▲ You can see columns and other paragraph arrangements

▲ You can see frames, graphics, headers and footers, and footnotes in position and edit them there

▲ You can see the actual layout of the page (e.g., margins and page edges)

▲ You have access to the ruler

▲ All material is visible

▲ All paragraph formatting is evident

▲ All proofing and enhancement tools are available

Disadvantages

The disadvantages of Page Layout view are:

▲ Scrolling can be slow

▲ The organization of the document is difficult to see

▲ Editing can be laborious

 **KEYBOARD SHORTCUT**

⌘-Option-P is the shortcut for Page Layout view.

 SEE ALSO

Part IV: Enhancing Your Work with Word 5's Special Features

Part VI: Printing Your Documents

THE NEW RIBBON AND IMPROVED RULER ▲

Word's *ribbon* and *ruler* greatly simplify many formatting tasks. New to Word 5, the ribbon provides many character enhancement tools, in addition to several shortcut buttons. The ruler's primary purpose is setting paragraph margins and tabs, but you can also use it to specify justification (right, left, double, or center) and line spacing, as well as to apply styles.

These two features are excellent examples of Word's practical flexibility: not only can you carry out many tasks with Word, but you often can accomplish any given task in several different ways. As we explore the ruler and ribbon, keep in mind that each function we discuss is really just one path to a particular end. Other paths to the same end are covered elsewhere in the book. In learning the advantages to each path, you will be mastering the program in the truest sense of the word.

Enhancing Text with the Ribbon

You may find it convenient to have the ribbon showing at all times (View ➤ Ribbon). It takes up very little room at the top of the screen, as illustrated in Figure II.6. Roughly

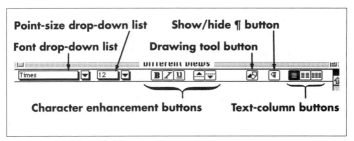

Figure II.6: The ribbon

speaking, the right third is devoted to three specialty features, while the other buttons and drop-down lists control character enhancement features.

We will cover the specialty features in more detail in other parts of the book. It is sufficient now for you to know that you can click the drawing tool button to reach Word's graphics editing window, the ¶ button to show or hide nonprinting characters, or one of the column buttons to reformat your text into multiple columns. Let's examine the other functions more closely.

 PROCEDURE

To change font and size from the ribbon, follow these steps:

1. Highlight the text you wish to change.

2. Click the down-pointing triangle on the font list.

3. Choose a font from the drop-down font menu and, if desired, a different size from the drop-down point-size menu. Alternatively, click in either box to highlight it.

Then, just type the font name or point size in the box and press Return. This is a handy way to change to a nonstandard font size.

PROCEDURE

To enhance text from the ribbon, highlight the text
you want to enrich and choose one of the buttons. You
have five choices:

▲ **Bold**

▲ *Italic*

▲ <u>Underline</u>

▲ Super^{s}cript

▲ Sub$_s$cript

 NOTE

Enhancements added from the ribbon use the default
settings. For instance, the underlining button adds continuous, single underline, while the superscript button
raises characters three points from the baseline. Also, the
buttons act as toggles: click once to turn a feature on;
click again to turn it off.

 KEYBOARD SHORTCUT

The shortcut for showing or hiding the ribbon is
⌘**-Option-R.**

SEE ALSO

Part III, Enhancing Text

Part III, Using Fonts Effectively

Part III, Columns—The Trick to Great Newsletters

Part IV, You as the Artist

Enhancing Paragraphs with the Ruler

While you might not want the ruler on-screen at all times (see Figure II.7), it certainly is helpful when you want to apply paragraph formatting. Selecting View ➤ Ruler toggles the ruler on or off.

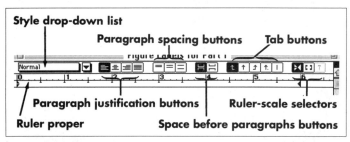

Figure II.7: The ruler

The ruler's paragraph enhancement buttons work the same as the ribbon's character enhancement buttons: you highlight what you want to alter, then click the button.

We'll save its more esoteric tab and margin functions, however, for *Part III*.

 KEYBOARD SHORTCUT

The shortcut for showing or hiding the ruler is ⌘-R.

BASICS

 **SEE ALSO**

Part III, Enhancing Styles

Part III, The Flow of Paragraphs

Part III, Moving Your Margins

Part III, Understanding Styles

OPENING A FILE FROM DISK ▲

Before we get into the nuts and bolts of editing, you'll need to learn how to retrieve files from disk. Like other basic Word functions, this is done with a simple menu command.

 PROCEDURE

To open a file from disk, choose File ➤ Open. A dialog box will appear, as shown in Figure II.8. Double-click on the desired file from the list. You can navigate

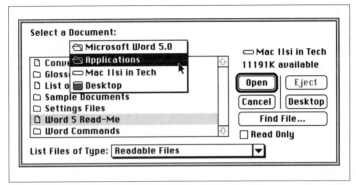

Figure II.8: The Open dialog box

your hard disk in this dialog box by clicking on the Desktop button or by clicking on the little folder icon at the top of the list and choosing from the drop-down menu.

KEYBOARD SHORTCUT

⌘**-O** is the shortcut to reach the Open dialog box.

Last-Four-Files Listing

This new Word 5 feature lists the last four documents you handled. It appends the file names to the File menu, near the bottom.

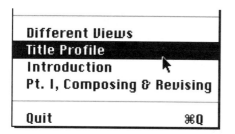

This can be extremely functional if you have a large number of files, because all you need to do to reopen a file is choose its name from the list. There is a caveat, though.

 NOTE

It is important to realize that this feature shows the last four files used, no matter *what* they were. So if you want to keep it private that you are working on documents such as *Toad-Sexing for Young Persons, My Amazing String Collection,* and *Some of My Closest Friends Are Crustaceans,* you may wish to deactivate this function.

 PROCEDURE

To activate or deactivate the last-four-files list, follow these steps.

1. Choose Tools ➤ Preferences.

2. Click on the View category.

3. Click to check or uncheck the option box for the List Recently Opened Documents option.

4. Close the Preferences dialog box.

Finding the Prodigal File

More and more, files are leaving home early to seek their fortunes. *O tempos, o mores!* Trouble is, when you want to find them, they're often in hiding. That's where Word 5's new Find File command can come in very handy.

 PROCEDURE

To locate a file with Find File, follow these steps:

1. Choose File ➤ Find File.

2. Type in and specify any pertinent information you can remember about the file, including text it contains (Any Text) and ranges of dates when you might have accessed (created or saved) the file. You can even modify which disks are searched. Note that the following fields rely on information entered into fields of the same name in the Summary Info dialog box:

   ▲ Title
   ▲ Subject
   ▲ Author

▲ Version

▲ Keywords

3. Click OK. Word will search for the file, apprising you of its success or failure.

 NOTE

Don't confuse this command with the System-7 desk accessory of the same name or with the File ➤ Find command in the Finder.

REVISING YOUR WORK

When we speak of "revising" a document, we mean one of the following:

▲ Adding material

▲ Deleting material

▲ Changing material

▲ Moving material

These activities are interrelated, but in exploring Word's functions, it's convenient to distinguish them. All editing techniques share this simple premise, though: before you can edit any material, you must either place the cursor or select (highlight) the material.

Highlighting Text

Highlighting text is usually easier with the mouse than the keyboard, although judicious use of the Shift key can help you select the exact text you want.

As explained in the section *Moving Around,* you select varying amounts of text, depending upon the number of times you click the mouse in the text window. (One click places the cursor; two clicks select a word; three clicks select a paragraph.) There is also a "hot zone" along the left margin of the text window, called the *selection bar.* To reach it, slide the mouse pointer toward the left edge of the screen; when you reach the selection bar, the pointer will change from an I-beam to a right-pointing arrow.

```
    "That's no cow!" shouted Edna, her mind racing.  But it
  was too late. The mooncalf had catapulted itself high into
  the air, all five legs spread deftly to act as a solar
  sail.
```

Selecting text is different here than in body text. Also, mouse clicks work differently in the selection bar.

Click...	*To*...
Once	Select a line
Twice	Select a paragraph
Three times	Select the entire document

Extending the Highlight

There are two analogous ways to extend the highlight: one relies on the mouse, the other on the Shift key.

PROCEDURE

To extend the highlight with the mouse, click the appropriate number of times, either within the text or in the selection bar. Do *not* release the mouse button after your last click, though. Then, simply drag the mouse, and the highlight will extend by discrete amounts. For instance, if you were to double-click within the text to select a word and then drag the mouse, the highlight would extend in one-word increments. If you were to click in the selection bar and drag the mouse, the highlight would extend in one-line increments. Release the mouse button only when you've finished selecting.

PROCEDURE

To extend the highlight with the keyboard, click the appropriate number of times, either within the text or in the selection bar. Then hold down Shift and click and drag the mouse. This method works exactly like the mouse method, except you must click to extend the highlight. In fact, if you are selecting text and forget to hold down the mouse button after clicking, don't waste time reselecting: just use the keyboard method instead!

NOTE

You can select text in columns by holding down Option while dragging with the mouse or extending the highlight with the Shift key. This is very useful in tabbed columns, but works equally well in regular text.

Cutting, Copying, and Pasting

Once you have highlighted some material, you can then take advantage of Word's Cut, Copy, and Paste functions.

 PROCEDURE

To cut highlighted material, choose Edit ➤ Cut. The material will be removed to the Clipboard. This is very useful when you want to paste it back in somewhere else. Generally, if you want to remove material from a document permanently, it is best to highlight it and hit the Delete key, rather than using the Cut command.

 KEYBOARD SHORTCUT

⌘-X is the shortcut for issuing the Cut command (F2 on extended keyboards).

 PROCEDURE

To copy highlighted material, choose Edit ➤ Copy. A copy of the material will be placed in the Clipboard, while the original is left untouched. (It will still be high-lighted, though, so if you were to type anything, the material would be erased.)

 **KEYBOARD SHORTCUT**

⌘-**C** is the shortcut for issuing the Copy command (F3 on extended keyboards).

 PROCEDURE

To paste text from the Clipboard, choose Edit ➤ Paste. A copy of the Clipboard's contents will be placed in your document at the cursor.

 KEYBOARD SHORTCUT

⌘-**V** is the shortcut for issuing the Paste command (F4 on extended keyboards).

 NOTE

Since both Cut and Copy place a copy of the material in the Clipboard, you can repeatedly paste in the same material. Also, you can cut or copy material from one document and paste it into another. There is a related command called Paste Special, which we will explore in detail in the *SnapGuide* to *Part IV.*

Drag-and-Drop Editing

Drag-and-drop editing is a new Word 5 feature. It is also a mixed blessing. The rationale behind drag-and-drop is that, since it's easier to cut and paste with the mouse, why not eliminate the need to give the Cut and Paste commands? While this works fine in theory, in practice there is one pitfall.

Drag-and-drop is not very helpful when you are just writing along. It's easy to forget that it's on and accidentally move material. When it's more useful is during a revision where you're moving material around a lot.

 PROCEDURE

To activate drag-and-drop editing, follow these steps:

1. Choose Tools ➤ Preferences.

2. The General Category (the default) should be showing.

3. Check the Drag-and-Drop Text Editing option.

4. Close the Preferences dialog box.

 PROCEDURE

To move material with drag-and-drop, follow these steps:

1. Highlight the material you want to move (see the sections *Moving Around* and *Highlighting Text*).

2. Click once on the highlighted material and hold down the mouse button. The pointer will change from a simple arrow to an arrow above a box. Notice also that the cursor changes to a dotted line.

> .ia, lici miliia ia.
>
> i catapulted it
>
> deftlv to act :

3. With the mouse button still depressed, move the pointer to place the blinking, dotted cursor where you want to reposition the material.

4. Release the mouse button. The material will move to its new position.

 NOTE

While dragging-and-dropping is functionally the same as cutting and pasting, a drag-and-drop does *not* copy the text to the Clipboard. Furthermore, you cannot drag-and-drop material from one document to another. (This leads to some *strange* results!) If you hold down ⌘ while doing a drag-and-drop, a *copy* of the material is moved—it works like a copy and paste.

Undoing and Repeating Edits

You can undo almost any edit you make in Word. While functions are a little more dodgy, you can undo many of them, too. You can even "undo" an undo; this lets you compare changes with originals to decide which you prefer. The Repeat command simply repeats your most recent edit.

PROCEDURE

To undo an edit, choose File ➤ Undo. Note that the actual name of this command varies, depending upon what you have just done. For example, if you have just been typing, the command will be called *Undo Typing*. If you have just pasted some text, the command will be *Undo Paste.*

 KEYBOARD SHORTCUT

⌘-**Z** keys the Undo command (F1 on extended keyboards).

 PROCEDURE

To repeat an edit, choose File ➤ Repeat. Note that, like the Undo command, the actual name of this command varies, depending upon what you have just done.

 KEYBOARD SHORTCUT

⌘-**Y** issues the Repeat command.

Finding and Replacing

One of the truly exciting new features in Word 5 is its ability to search for and replace formatting. The program has always had good Find and Replace functions, which are undeniably useful, but Word 5's Find and Replace are a quantum leap ahead of Word 4's. These features alone might convince many people to upgrade.

Finding and replacing are very similar operations. You use Find to locate a particular word, phrase, or character. To replace text, you find it first and then substitute what's there with a new word, phrase, or character. So Find is really a subset of Replace.

 PROCEDURE

To find a particular word, phrase, or character, follow these steps:

1. Choose Edit ➤ Find. The Find dialog box will appear, as shown in Figure II.9.

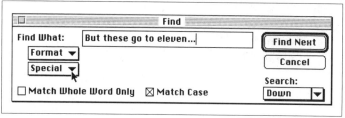

Figure II.9: The Find dialog box

2. Type in the word, phrase, or character you want to find. (Note that you can select nonprinting and other characters from the Special drop-down menu: this allows you to search for such adumbrage as optional hyphens.)

3. Optionally, choose a command from the Format drop-down menu.

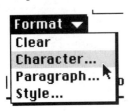

These bring up dialog boxes we will discuss in other parts of the book. You use these dialog boxes to specify the format you wish to include in, or exclude from, the search criteria. Alternatively, you can click on a button on the ribbon. Any formatting you specify will be noted below the Find What box. If you want to clear any formatting, choose Clear from the Format menu.

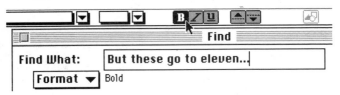

4. Click Find Next repeatedly to find all occurrences of the text in your document. You can close the box, click Cancel, or click in the text window at any time to abandon your search.

NOTE

The Find dialog box has several useful options.

▲ Match Whole Word Only limits the search to only those occurrences of the specified text that are whole words. For example, with this option enabled, a search for *bid* would find only *bid,* not *rabid, abide,* or *forbidden.*

▲ Match Case ensures that only those occurrences that match the case of the sample text will be flagged. Case will not matter if this is unchecked.

▲ Finally, you can search a document either Down (toward the end) or Up (toward the beginning). This can be handy if you have a long document.

 KEYBOARD SHORTCUT

⌘-**F** executes the Find command.

 PROCEDURE

To replace a particular word, phrase, or character, follow the steps given above for the Find command, but choose Edit ➤ Replace instead of Edit ➤ Find. The execution is essentially the same, only now you must fill in both the Find What and Replace With boxes. (The Format and Special menus can be useful when specifying formats or special characters.) Then, either click Replace

All to replace all occurrences, or click Find Next and then Replace to verify each substitution manually.

KEYBOARD SHORTCUT

⌘-**H** invokes the Replace command.

SEE ALSO

Part III, Enhancing Text

Part III, The Flow of Paragraphs

Part III, Understanding Styles

PRINTING

There are many subtleties to printing, especially if you want to realize certain special effects. But Word's default print settings are well conceived, and it is worthwhile to know the basic print command.

PROCEDURE

To print the active document, choose File ➤ Print and click Print to accept the default settings.

KEYBOARD SHORTCUT

⌘-P is the shortcut to print a document.

NOTE

Before you print, be sure to *check the Chooser* to ensure your computer is connected to the right printer. (The name of the printer will also appear at the top of the Print dialog box.) I can't count the number of times I have blissfully sent a document off to print, only to have it trundle out of some decrepit, smuggled laser printer in Irkutsk, Siberia. Fortunately, my friend Genna ships my hardcopies back to me COD.

BASICS

SEE ALSO

Part VI: Printing Your Documents

HELP!

Word's help facility is both accessible and clear. Simply choose Window ➤ Help, and you've opened the portals to a gigantic (416K) help file. Size notwithstanding, Help is easy to navigate.

 **KEYBOARD SHORTCUT**

To get context-sensitive help right from the keyboard, simply press the **Help** key and click the question-mark icon on the feature you wish to learn about. (If you are in the middle of an operation, you'll get help about it.) If you don't have an extended keyboard and find yourself seeking help often, press ⌘-/.

BALLOON HELP ▲

If you've never used Word, Balloon Help can be a god-send for about twelve seconds. Unfortunately, this new System-7 feature is *too* helpful: every part of the screen brings up a new balloon. In a short time, you'll probably be happy if you never see another balloon again in your life.

 PROCEDURE

To subject yourself to Balloon Help, choose Show Balloons from the Balloon Help menu. As you move the pointer over various areas of the screen, you'll see felicitous comic-strip balloons describing Word's features.

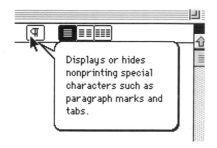

To rid yourself of Balloon Help, choose Hide Balloons from the Balloon Help menu.

QUITTING WORD

When you conclude a Word session, it's a good idea to quit Word, if for no other reason than to see whether any support files are unsaved. Like most Mac programs, if there are any documents with unsaved changes when you quit, you are given the option to save those changes. But, most people don't forget to save their documents; it's much more likely they'll forget to save changes to glossaries, dictionaries, and such. Furthermore, there are certain settings that are permanently saved *only* when you quit Word (e.g., commands and preferences). The quit command is File ➤ Quit.

KEYBOARD SHORTCUT

⌘-**Q** is the shortcut for quitting Word.

SNAPGUIDE TO WRITING ▲

No matter what anyone tells you, writing is at bottom just plain hard work. In fact, the more effortless you want your writing to *appear,* the harder you'll have to work at it. But there are both fruitful and inept ways to spend your energy. In this SnapGuide, I will explain how you can apply Word 5's unique tools to maximize your efforts.

Use the Outliner

Anything that prevents you from putting pen to paper (or fingers to keyboard) is a distraction. In writing, most distractions are psychological: People think, "I don't have anything to say" or "I can't get my thoughts organized." Well, I say, get them organized! Order your ideas, and composition will follow.

Word's outlining feature can be a big help in corralling your thoughts. While an exhaustive tutorial on the outliner is beyond the scope of this book, it is worthwhile to discuss the basics. Follow this example.

Let's say you have to write a stockholder's report on your company's goals for the next six months. This can be daunting: not only do you not know whom to talk to, you don't know what questions you'd ask them. So let's organize your thoughts with Word 5's outliner. It doesn't take too much imagination to come up with these four very general goals (they could apply to any company):

▲ Increase productivity and sales

▲ Maintain quality control

▲ Increase employee satisfaction

▲ Decrease employee absenteeism (due to illness and stress)

To put Word to work for you, simply type these four goals into a new document, switch to Outline view, and make them all first-level heads.

 PROCEDURE

To make regular text into a heading, just place the cursor in the text and click the leftmost icon (left-pointing arrow) on the outline bar.

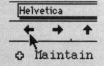

Next, go to the end of the first line, press return, and click the demote-head level icon (the right-pointing arrow).

This turns whatever you type into a second level head. As-suming the first heading was *Increase productivity and sales,* you might then enter the following, more specific lines:

▲ Purchase new equipment

▲ Evaluate current procedures

▲ Evaluate current marketing scheme

Now you're getting somewhere. You could in turn make lower-level heads beneath each of these secondary heads, but at this point, you should already be getting an idea of whom to talk to about these subcategories. For in-stance, evaluating the current marketing scheme would fall under the purview of the head of marketing. Go talk to him or her and get the lowdown on what's being planned. Let's say marketing intends to:

▲ Revamp their current crop of magazine ads

▲ Promote a new video-marketing campaign

▲ Hire a high-profile celebrity to hawk products on TV

Make these your third-level heads.

Follow the above steps for all your first- and second-level heads, and your report's structure will materialize quickly. Then change to Normal view and start writing the actual details.

Don't worry if you "can't write" or if you've never writ-ten before: If you can *think,* you can *write.* And with Word, because you can revise your work endlessly, you *can* be a good writer.

There Is No Writing, Just Rewriting

John Updike, in trying to explain his elusive craft, once said, "There is no writing, just rewriting." No writer gets it "perfect" the first time, so don't feel like a half-wit if you don't either.

Believe me: *Everyone* needs an editor. I'm not just saying that because I am one. The truth is, it's very hard to put your thoughts down accurately. That is why it is so important to get your thoughts on paper. *The crafting of words occurs after they are written.* This might be the single most useful tip I can give you. Get your ideas down, then edit them.

Word 5 can be a powerful ally in crafting your writing. Use the spell checker, grammar checker, and thesaurus (discussed in detail in *Part V: Proofing: The Finishing Touches*), and I guarantee you will improve your writing noticeably.

PART

FORMATTING
FOR GREAT RESULTS

To properly understand formatting in Word 5, we must keep in mind several different perspectives. Character formatting enhances individual words. Paragraph formatting, which enriches paragraphs, also affects the impact of formatted characters—you must keep both in mind. Finally, page or document formatting requires that you consider not only the design of your pages, but also the ways in which it influences the effect of your character and paragraph formatting.

Although it is wise to format your documents in this order—from character to page—it is not essential. Also, developing a sense of what your pages will look like can help you make good decisions about character formatting. See the *SnapGuide* for this part for more details.

ENHANCING TEXT ▲

In addition to supporting hundreds of fonts (covered in the section *Using Fonts Effectively*), Word provides you with a wealth of text enhancement options. They fall neatly into three categories: styles, underlining, and kerning.

Character Styles

Not to be confused with paragraph styles, *character styles* include those shown in Figure III.1.

plain	**Bold**
Italic	Outline
Shadow	Strikethru
SMALL CAPS	ALL CAPS

Figure III.1: Word's seven character enhancement styles

KEYBOARD SHORTCUT

⌘-**D** is the shortcut for opening the Character dialog box. Also, double-clicking on the ribbon will open this dialog box.

PROCEDURE

To apply a character style, follow these steps:

1. Select the text you wish to enhance.

2. Choose Format ➤ Character.

3. Click on each style you wish to apply.

4. Click OK. Alternatively, to see how your enhancements will look before they take effect, you can click Apply. Then if you don't like what you see, you can simply deselect the styles before clicking OK.

 NOTE

If you click the Apply button, but your changes are hidden by the Styles dialog box, you can drag the dialog box out of the way.

 KEYBOARD SHORTCUT

Here are keyboard shortcuts (all toggle commands) for applying the styles shown in Figure III.1:

Style	*Shortcut*
Bold	⌘-B
Italic	⌘-I
Outline	⌘-Shift-D
Shadow	⌘-Shift-W
Strikethru	⌘-Shift-/
Small Caps	⌘-Shift-H
All Caps	⌘-Shift-K
Plain text	⌘-Shift-Z

NOTE

You can quickly add bold and italic formatting by selecting text and clicking the correct button on the ribbon.

Obviously, not every style is appropriate to serious writing. For instance, outline and shadow are what typesetters think of as *display styles*; that is, they would use them only for a particular effect, usually in a heading. Strikethru, too, is clearly not a style you would use to enhance an important point. The plain-text shortcut is useful if you wish to remove several styles at once.

NOTE

There is one other style, hidden, but it is better not to think of this as a text style. It is more of a stipulation, inasmuch as it determines whether text will appear when the document is printed.

Color

Colors serve the same purpose as styles: they highlight important text. Unfortunately, even though many people have color monitors, most do not have color printers. Thus, the benefits of color are limited.

However, keep in mind a simple but often-ignored axiom: on-screen enhancements are just as legitimate as printed ones. Distinguishing on-screen text more clearly is a defensible reason to use any enhancement you like. For example, if you have difficulty seeing boldfaced text on-screen, you can make all your boldfaced text red, blue, green, or some other vivid color. To do this, use the Edit ➤ Replace command, as discussed in *Part I, Finding and Replacing*, with the following settings:

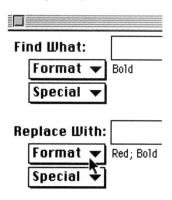

Even if you don't have a color printer or monitor, you can save text with color enhancements. Then, if you later have access to a color printer, you can print out the colors.

 PROCEDURE

To change the color of highlighted text, choose Format ➤ Character and select a color from the Color drop-down list.

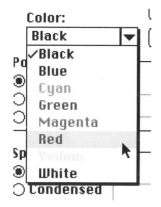

Then click Apply or OK to see the effect. Any colors you add to text will not affect its printed appearance, so long as you do *not* choose the Color/Grayscale option when you print.

Casing

There is a nifty new feature in Word 5 called Change Case. This command offers you five different casing options. If you've ever typed a document only to find out the upper- and lowercase choices you made in, say, headings were wrong, you can appreciate how useful this tool is.

PROCEDURE

To change the casing of highlighted text, choose Format ➤ Change Case. A dialog box will pop up. Choose the desired casing and click OK.

```
╔═══════════════════ Change Case ═══════════════════╗
║  ⦿ UPPERCASE            ┌─────────────┐            ║
║  ○ lowercase            │     OK      │            ║
║  ○ Title Case           └─────────────┘            ║
║  ○ Sentence case.       ┌─────────────┐            ║
║  ○ tOGGLE cASE          │   Cancel    │            ║
║                         └─────────────┘            ║
╚════════════════════════════════════════════════════╝
```

Underlining

Another way to enhance text is through *underlining*.
Word offers you four underlining choices.

<u>Single underline</u>   <u>Word</u> <u>underline</u>

<u>Double underline</u>   <u>Dotted underline</u>

It is often more elegant to italicize text than to underline it. In fact, true underlining is quite rare in published
books. You will probably find that your documents look
professional if you use italics, but there are always creative uses for any kind of enhancement. For example,
dotted or double underlining may work well in a document heading.

 PROCEDURE

To apply underlining, follow these steps:

1. Highlight the text you wish to underline.

2. Choose Format ➤ Character.

3. Select the underline style you want from the Underline drop-down list.

4. Click OK. To view the underline before putting it into effect, click Apply.

NOTE

You can also click on the underline button in the ribbon to apply or remove continuous, single underline.

KEYBOARD SHORTCUT

⌘-U is the shortcut for adding continuous, single underline.

Kerning

Adjusting the space between characters is called *kerning*. It is usually measured in *points*. While Word does not have the kerning flexibility of PageMaker or QuarkXPress, clever use of its Condensed and Expanded settings can produce some impressive effects.

PROCEDURE

To adjust the space between characters, follow these steps:

1. Highlight the text you wish to kern.

2. Choose Format ➤ Character.

3. Select either Expanded or Condensed in the spacing box.

4. Specify a distance in the By box.

5. Click OK or click Apply to see the effect before you apply it.

Experience will show you what distances in the By box work best with which fonts. Word's defaults, though, look fairly decent for most fonts.

Normal spacing

Condensed spacing (1.5 pts)

E x p a n d e d   s p a c i n g   (3   p t s)

 NOTE

In the context of kerning, you should understand the difference between *monospace* and *proportional* typefaces. In monospace fonts, each letter takes up exactly the same amount of space; for instance, a capital *W* takes up no more room than a lowercase *i*. Clearly, though, this is a waste of space. That's why many people prefer proportional fonts, where each letter takes up a different amount of space, depending upon its width. To make your documents look professional, it's best to choose a proportional font such as Times, Palatino, or Helvetica.

USING FONTS EFFECTIVELY ▲

Word 5 is 100-percent compatible with System 7's new *TrueType* fonts. Unlike the old *bitmap* fonts, TrueType fonts are *scalable.* This means that you need only a single file of a particular font to create it in *any* size on screen or in printouts. With bitmap fonts, you needed each point size you wanted, both in your System Folder and on your printer. The only disadvantages of TrueType fonts are that they take up a lot of memory and are more expensive than bitmaps.

No matter what kind of fonts you have installed on your Mac, Word can access them all. You can think of fonts as additional text enhancement options.

 PROCEDURE

To change the font of highlighted text, you have four choices:

▲ Choose the font you want from the Font menu.

▲ Choose Format ➤ Character and select a font from the drop-down Font list.

▲ Type ⌘-Shift-E. You'll notice the word *Font* high-lighted in the status area (in the lower-left corner of document windows).

Type the name of the font you want and press Return.

▲ Use the ribbon. See *Part I, Enhancing Text with the Ribbon* for details on this method.

 NOTE

While even a gloss of page layout principles is beyond the scope of this book, you should be aware of the difference between serif and sans serif fonts and learn a few guidelines for mixing fonts. This information appears in the *SnapGuide* to *Part III.*

Point Size

The actual sizes of characters are measured in *points* (pt). A point is approximately 1/72"—a 12-pt character is 1/6" high. The clarity and uniformity of a given font at different point sizes depends upon whether the font is a bitmap or TrueType font (see above).

PROCEDURE

To change the point size of selected text, you have the
same options you had when changing the font (see
above), except there is no shortcut for changing point
size in the status area. In addition, you can choose Up or
Down on the Font menu to change the size of the font.

KEYBOARD SHORTCUT

⌘-[decreases the type size by 1 pt and ⌘-] increases
the type size by 1 pt. You will see the size in the status
area in the lower-left corner of document windows.

NOTE

There are no limits (other than practicality and sanity)
on the point size you can use.

Superscript and Subscript

Mathematicians and other scientists will appreciate
Word's super- and subscripting features. Among their
other uses, these commands are great for showing ex-
ponentials and scientific notation for molecules.

```
Potassium sulfate (K2SO4) can be great fun at pool parties...
```

```
The Pythagorean theorum, which states that a2+b2=c2, is...
```

There is one important term you should know when discussing scripts: baseline. The *baseline* of a line of text is the imaginary boundary that the bottoms of most letters rest upon. Some letters—*p*, *q*, and *y*, for instance—have *descenders*. These are the parts of the letters that drop below the baseline. When you superscript a letter, you are raising it above the baseline; when you subscript, you are dropping the letter below the baseline.

 PROCEDURE

To super- or subscript a selected character, you have three options:

▲ Choose Format ➤ Character and click on either the Superscript or Subscript option in the Position box. Then enter the distance you want the character raised or dropped from the baseline and click OK or Apply.

▲ Use the keyboard shortcuts, ⌘-**Shift**- + for superscript and ⌘-**Shift**- − for subscript.

▲ Use the ribbon. See *Part I, Enhancing Text with the Ribbon* for details on this method.

 NOTE

If you use either the ribbon or the Character dialog box to script a character, it remains the same point size. However, if you use the keyboard shortcuts, the character is automatically dropped one standard point size (e.g., from 12 pts to 10, from 18 pts to 14, etc.) This can be very useful, because it is customary to show super- and subscripts in a *smaller* point size than text.

SEE ALSO

Part IV, Equation Editor

THE FLOW OF PARAGRAPHS

Word defines a paragraph as anything followed by a paragraph marker (¶). A paragraph's format is stored with its paragraph mark. For example, in Figure III.2, the first paragraph mark stores the formatting for the head; the second, the formatting for the body text; and the third, the formatting for the graphic.

Paragraph enhancements are often not as easy to see as character enhancements. Also, their effects are usually more subtle. But if *you* disregard the appearance of your paragraphs, you can be sure your *readers* will notice the difference. As with character styles, you must first select the text you wish to change. This means either placing the cursor somewhere in a single paragraph or selecting portions of multiple paragraphs.

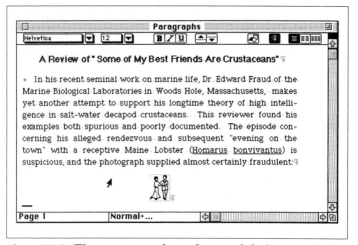

Figure III.2: Three paragraph markers and their respective paragraphs

Tabbing

The body-text paragraph in Figure III.2 begins with a *tab indent.* It is indicated by the small, right-pointing arrow.

NOTE

It is customary but not requisite to begin paragraphs with an indent; if you don't use indents, be sure to add extra space between paragraphs.

PROCEDURE

To indent a paragraph using tabs, simply press the Tab key at the start of each new paragraph. There is a trick you can do with margins to effect automatic indents: see the section *Indenting* below.

Changing the Default Tabs

Word's default tabs (one every ½") are adequate for most applications. You can change them, though, if you find that they don't suit your needs. To do this, you use the ruler.

You have five tab styles to choose from: left-aligned, centered, right-aligned, decimal, and vertical bar. They are illustrated in Figure III.3.

FORMATTING

```
Left-aligned          Right-aligned
     Vertical bar        Centered      Decimal
                    Tab Styles

  Normal
  0      1       2      3      4      5      6

          Major League Players Eligible for Arbitration

   Player          Position      Age     Salary (in millions)
   G. Carter          C          38           5.4
   E. Davis          OF          28          10.278
   M. Gallego        2B          31           5.5
   E. Murray         1B          37           4.33
   B. Saberhagen     P           26           7.2
   D. Tartabull      OF          27           9.62

  Page 1              Normal+...
```

Figure III.3: The five tab styles

As you can see, you can use tabs for simple multi-column lists like the one shown in Figure III.3. For more complicated lists, particularly those where entries run over to several lines, it is better to use Word's Table feature. See *Part IV, Setting Up Tables* for more information.

 PROCEDURE

To add new tabs to the ruler, highlight the paragraphs you want affected, click on one of the five tab options in the ruler,

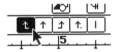

and click in the ruler proper where you want to place the new tab.

NOTE

Any tabs you add to the ruler erase all *default* tabs to the left of the new one. (Tabs *you* have added to the left of the new one will remain untouched, though.) To specify exactly where to place new tabs, just double-click on a tab and type the exact position in the Tabs dialog box.

PROCEDURE

To move an existing tab, click on it and drag it to its
new location.

Tab Leaders

You've probably seen *tab leaders* before and not known it.
They are the dotted or dashed lines in between items
separated by tabs. In long lists, they aid in reading across
space that would otherwise be blank. Word offers three
kinds of tab leader:

No leader   page 5
Dotted leader ....page 17
Dashed leader -------------------------page 101
Solid leader_____ page 122

These lines might be difficult to read without leaders;
tightly packed text, like phone directory listings, would
be nearly impossible.

PROCEDURE

To add tab leaders to selected paragraphs, you have
two options:

▲ Choose Format ➤ Paragraph and click the Tabs
button. If hidden, the ruler will appear. In the
ruler, click the tab you want to add the leader to
(a leader is controlled by the tab that follows it).
Double-click the type of leader you want in the
Tabs dialog box,

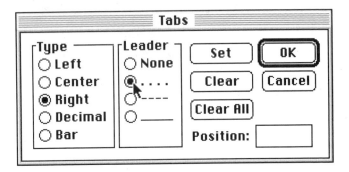

and click OK to close the Paragraph dialog box.

▲ Show the ruler if it's hidden. Double-click the tab in the ruler to bring up the Tabs dialog box. Double-click the type of leader you want. Click OK.

 KEYBOARD SHORTCUT

⌘-**M** is the shortcut for bringing up the Paragraph dialog box. Also double-clicking many (but not all) of the elements on the ruler—including the alignment and spacing buttons, the indents themselves, and the top half of the ruler proper—will bring up this dialog box.

Indenting

Often confused with margins, *indents* are the space between text and margins. Usually you indent only the first line of a paragraph, although there are applications where you might indent a whole paragraph. (When showing block quotes, it is customary to use both left and right indents.) You can change a paragraph's indents either with the ruler or from the Paragraph dialog box. Let's examine both methods.

 PROCEDURE

To adjust indents with the ruler, follow these steps:

1. Highlight the paragraphs you wish to change.

2. Make sure the ruler scale is set to indents. You can tell by looking at the ruler-scale selector. The left button should be highlighted.

3. Click and drag either the right- or left-indent marker on the ruler to reposition it.

4. If you wish an additional first-line indent, drag the top half of the left-indent marker to the right.

PROCEDURE

To adjust indents with the Paragraph dialog box, follow these steps:

1. Highlight the paragraphs you wish to change.

2. Choose Format ➤ Paragraph. The Paragraph dialog box will appear.

3. Change the Left, Right, and First (first-line) settings in the Indentation area.

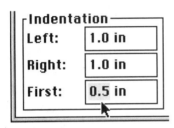

4. Click Apply to see how your changes will look and then click OK.

Hanging Indents

Hanging indents are a nifty variation on the indent theme. These are paragraphs where all the text is indented *except* the first line. These make numbered and bulleted lists look really snazzy, as shown in Figure III.4.

1. Hanging indents are really noticeable when the text runs over to several lines.	• Hanging indents are really noticeable when the text runs over to several lines.
2. Otherwise, you can't tell that they are hanging indents.	• Otherwise, you can't tell that they are hanging indents.
3. Even so, it is a good idea to format lists with hanging indents, so if you add any text later, it will automatically indent to the right place.	• Even so, it is a good idea to format lists with hanging indents, so if you add any text later, it will automatically indent to the right place.

Figure III.4: Numbered and bulleted lists with hanging indents

PROCEDURE

To create a hanging indent, follow these steps:

1. Highlight the paragraphs you wish to change.

2. Check the ruler-scale selector to make sure the mode is indents.

3. Hold down Shift; then click and drag the lower half of the left-indent marker to reposition it.

Then, just remember to hit Tab after your number or bullet before you start typing your text.

Aligning Text

Word provides four text alignment options: left, center, right, and double-justified. They are shown in Figure III.5.

LEFT-ALIGNED

Lorem ipsum dolor sit amet, consectetuer adipiscing elit sed diam nonummy nibh euismod tincidunt ut laoreet dolore vui aliquam erat volutpat. Ut wisi enim ad minim veniam, quis nostrud exerci tation ullamcorper suscipit lobortis nisl ut mor commodo consequat. Duis te feugifaccilisi et dignissimar

CENTERED

Lorem ipsum dolor sit amet, consectetuer adipiscing elit sed diam nonummy nibh euismod tincidunt ut laoreet dolore vui aliquam erat volutpat. Ut wisi enim ad minim veniam, quis nostrud exerci tation ullamcorper suscipit lobortis nisl ut mor commodo consequat. Duis te feugifaccilisi et

RIGHT-ALIGNED

Lorem ipsum dolor sit amet, consectetuer adipiscing elit sed diam nonummy nibh euismod tincidunt ut laoreet dolore vui aliquam erat volutpat. Ut wisi enim ad minim veniam, quis nostrud exerci tation ullamcorper suscipit lobortis nisl ut mor commodo consequat. Duis te feugifaccilisi et dignissimar

DOUBLE-JUSTIFIED

Lorem ipsum dolor sit amet, consectetuer adipiscing elit sed diamne nonummy nibh euismod tincidint ut laoteet dolore vui aliquam erat volutpad Ut wisi enim ad minim veniam, quis nostrud exerci tation ullamcorper suscip lobortis nisl ut mor commodo consequat. Duis te feugifaccilisi et dignissimart blandit praesent luptatum voila.

Figure III.5: Word's four paragraph alignment options

PROCEDURE

To set the alignment for a paragraph, choose the paragraphs you wish to change and click one of the four paragraph alignment buttons on the ruler.

 KEYBOARD SHORTCUT

These are the keyboard shortcuts for changing the alignment:

Left	⌘-Shift-L
Center	⌘-Shift-C
Right	⌘-Shift-R
Double-justified	⌘-Shift-J

Numbering Lines and Paragraphs

Lawyers will like Word's line-numbering options. Numbered paragraphs, too, have their uses: as you may have noticed, all of the numbered lists in this book are really numbered paragraphs.

PROCEDURE

To enable automatic line numbering, follow these steps:

1. Choose Format ➤ Section.

2. Click on the Line Numbers button.

3. Specify how Word should handle the numbering in the Line Numbers area. (By Page restarts each page with 1; By Section starts each section with 1; Continuous numbers the lines continuously through the document; and Off removes line numbering.)

4. Click OK in both the Line Numbers and Section dialog boxes.

 NOTE

You can see line numbers only in Print Preview and on printed output. If the numbers are getting cut off when you print, go back to the Line Numbers dialog box and adjust the setting in the From Text box. This specifies how close the numbers should print to your text.

 PROCEDURE

To number paragraphs, follow these steps:

1. Highlight the paragraphs you wish to number. This is very important—if you forget to do this, you'll probably want to use Undo immediately, because Word will number *every* paragraph in your document.

2. Choose Tools ➤ Renumber.

3. In the Format box, specify the format you want. The default is *n.* followed by a tab, where *n* is a number that increases by increments of 1. If you'd prefer to have a space instead of a tab, just type **1.** followed by a space. If you want to start with a number other than 1, specify it in the Start at box.

4. Click OK.

 NOTE

You can use the Renumber command on paragraphs that already have numbers. This is extremely helpful when you have a long numbered list and need to add an additional item to the list. The Renumber command saves you from doing the renumbering by hand.

Leading

The space between lines of text is called the *leading*. Like kerning, leading is measured in points. Word's default line spacing is single space, which provides the line leading appropriate for the size of the font. For example, a 12-pt font would have roughly 12-pt leading. You can change the leading either with the ruler or in the Paragraph dialog box.

PROCEDURE

To change the leading with the ruler, highlight the paragraphs you want to change and click one of the three line-spacing buttons on the ruler.

If you double-click one of the buttons, the Paragraph dialog box appears and you can specify the leading more precisely, as discussed next.

 PROCEDURE

To change the leading with the Paragraph dialog box, select the paragraphs, choose Format ➤ Paragraph, and specify the leading in the Line box. Then click OK.

The Space Before and After

Besides changing the line spacing, you can also specify space before or after paragraph breaks. You might give headings some additional space after to set them off from body text. Space before helps readability if you've elected not to indent paragraphs.

 PROCEDURE

To set the space before or after, follow these steps:

1. Highlight the text you want affected.

2. Choose Format ➤ Paragraph.

3. Enter the amount of space you want in either the Before or After box.

4. Click OK.

KEYBOARD SHORTCUT

⌘-**Shift-O** is the shortcut for achieving 12 pts of space before the selected paragraphs. This is a toggle command.

NOTE

A quick way to specify space before is to click on the space before the ¶ button in the ruler.

This inserts 12 pts of space before each new paragraph. To remove this space, click the other button—the no space before the ¶ button.

Page Breaks

Sometimes you can improve the look of a document by forcing a page break. Word automatically paginates documents, but not with an eye for aesthetics. For example, headings look lousy if they come right at the bottom of the page, but this is exactly what Word does on occasion.

Wait until you are completely finished with your document (including spelling and hyphenation), though, before forcing a page break. Text flows around *soft* page breaks (ones that Word inserts) but not around *hard* or *manual* page breaks. An ill-advised manual page break can have some unintended effects (such as pages with only a few lines on them).

 PROCEDURE

To force a page break, place the cursor where you want the page to break and choose Insert ➤ Page Break (or press Shift-Enter).

CREATING AND USING STYLES

You might be wondering whether there is some way to store several character and paragraph enhancements together as a set. There is, and it is called a *style.* Styles take a little time to learn, but a small investment in time now will pay high dividends later.

 PROCEDURE

To create styles, follow these steps:

   1. Select the text that you want to format.

2. Choose Format ➤ Style. The Style: *document name* dialog box will appear, as shown in Figure III.6.

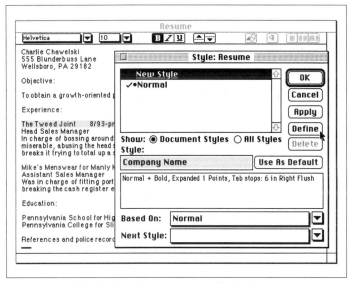

Figure III.6: The Style: *document name* dialog box

3. Specify any text or paragraph formats that you want the style to reflect. You can use the ribbon, ruler, and dialog box tricks explained earlier in this part in the sections *Enhancing Text* and *The Flow of Paragraphs.* Then enter a name for your style.

4. At this point, it might be a good idea to click Apply to see the effect of your style. Click Define.

5. If you want to author another style based upon the one you've just created, simply click New Style in the list, give the new style a name, and add the formatting you want. (Don't forget to click Define!)

6. Click OK to close the box.

 KEYBOARD SHORTCUT

⌘-T is the keyboard shortcut for opening the Style dialog box.

Now you'll see the elegant utility of styles. The resume shown in Figure III.6 listed company names. Here's how you would apply the Company Name style.

 PROCEDURE

To apply a style, follow these steps:

1. Select the text you want to apply the style to.

2. Choose Format ➤ Style.

3. Double-click on the name of the style you want to apply.

The text will change to reflect the style, as shown in Figure III.7.

 NOTE

On the left side of the ruler is the style drop-down list. This works very much like the font drop-down list

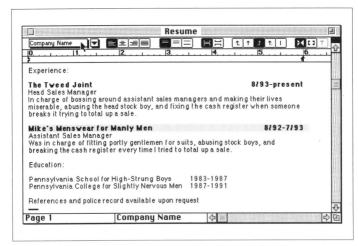

Figure III.7: Applying styles can save time and ensure consistency

on the ribbon. It is a shortcut for selecting styles. To use it, simply select the text you want to change and choose the style you want from the drop-down list.

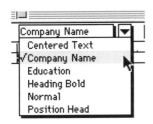

By using the tools described in this section, I was able to format the resume, as shown in Figure III.8, in about two minutes.

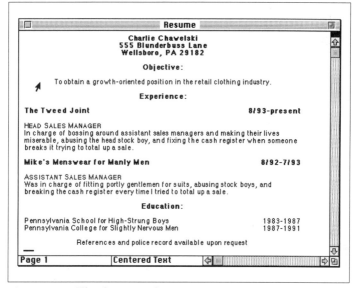

Figure III.8: The formatted resume

The real power of styles becomes apparent when you want to edit a style. When you make changes to a style (for instance, changing the leading of a heading style), all text formatted with that style automatically changes to reflect your new settings.

 PROCEDURE

To edit a style, choose Format ➤ Styles. Click on the style you want to change in the Styles dialog box. Make your alterations. When you're finished, click Define to record your changes.

USING THE GLOSSARY

Word's *glossary* is a list of text and graphics entries that people often like to insert in their documents. These include the date, the page number, the name of a file, and the author. There is no actual text in a glossary entry, just a command that tells Word "insert today's date," or "insert the author's name."

You can even use dynamic glossary entries. These actually keep track of the date, the page number, and so on, such that if you were to print a file several days after you finished it, the date of printing would appear on the printed version. One use for this feature is to insert the *print date* glossary command in your letterhead stationery file. Then the correct date will print on all your letters.

In addition to Word's standard, variable glossary entries, you can add entries of your own. You might, for instance, create an entry for the name of your company or of a product. Then you wouldn't have to type them in.

  PROCEDURE

To define a glossary entry, follow these steps:

1. Highlight the material (including text and graphics) you want to define as an entry. If you want to copy paragraph formatting, copy the paragraph mark (¶).

2. Choose Edit ➤ Glossary.

111

3. Type a name for your entry in the Name box and click Define. Your new entry will appear in the list. Click Close to banish the dialog box.

 NOTE

If you define a glossary and then later cannot find it in the Glossary dialog box, it may be that Word is showing only its standard glossary entries. To see your entries, click the User Entries option.

 PROCEDURE

To insert a glossary entry into a document, choose Edit ➤ Glossary and simply double-click on the entry you want. It will appear at the cursor. If you don't see entries you've assigned, click on the User Entries option.

 PROCEDURE

To add a glossary entry to the Work menu, choose Edit ➤ Glossary, press ⌘-Option- +, and click on the item you want to add, as shown in Figure III.9. Close the dialog box.

 NOTE

In addition to glossary entries, you can add documents and styles to the Work menu. To do so, press ⌘-Option- +

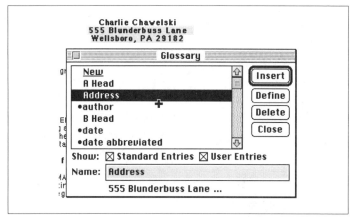

Figure III.9: Click on the entry you wish to add to the Work menu

and click on the item you wish to add. **Warning:** Do not try to add any of the items in the ruler or ribbon. This will cause your Mac to bomb. (I learned this the hard way.) When you quit Word after making changes to your glossary, you'll be given a chance to save your changes.

KEYBOARD SHORTCUT

The shortcut for accessing the Glossary dialog box is ⌘-K.

SEE ALSO

Part II, Stationery

Part VI, A Kinder, Gentler Print Merge

DIVIDING A DOCUMENT INTO SECTIONS ▲

Before getting into the nitty-gritty of page formatting, you must understand the concept of sections. A *section* is a collection of text elements that, at least for the purposes of page layout, act as a unit. A section can be as little as one paragraph—the banner head at the top of a newsletter—or as much as an entire document.

To vary page layout components (location of footnotes, columns, page numbers, headers, footers, and list numbers) within a single document, you *must* break the document up into sections. While text formatting can change from one word to the next, and paragraph formatting from one paragraph to the next, section formatting decisions govern whole sections.

There are many reasons why you might break a document into sections. Here are a few of the more common ones:

▲ You are writing a report with several parts and want each part's footnote numbering to restart at 1.

▲ You want to include a two- or three-column passage of text in the middle of a single-column document.

▲ In a multipart report, you want the headers and footers to vary from part to part.

PROCEDURE

To break a document into sections, place the cursor where you want the section to break and choose Insert ➤ Section Break (or press ⌘-Enter).

 NOTE

While sections are ideal for certain purposes, there are times when it's better to break a single document (i.e., file) into several documents rather than simply subdividing it into sections:

▲ Several people are working on different parts of the same document.

▲ The document is becoming very long. (With documents over about 50 pages, many of Word's functions become noticeably sluggish.)

MOVING YOUR MARGINS

Margins are the blank areas between the text or graphics in your document and the edge of the paper they're to be printed on. Word's default left and right margins are 1¼", acceptable for most contingencies. There may be times, though, when you want to squeeze a lot of text on a page; to do so, you can change the margins. It's best, for example, to limit resumes to one page. You'd be surprised how much information you can cram onto a

FORMATTING

single page if you know a few tricks. See the *SnapGuide* for Part V for details.

There are three methods for changing margins: with the ruler, in the Document dialog box, and in Print Preview.

NOTE

It is best not to try to effect formatting by using the margins. For instance, if you want a block quote to have wider margins than the text before and after it, it is better to change the indents than to fiddle about with the margins: changing the margins for one paragraph resets them for *all* material in the same document.

PROCEDURE

To change your margins with the ruler, click on the middle button of the ruler-scale selector

and drag the left- or right-margin marker to the desired location.

NOTE

The ruler method allows you to change only the left and right margins. To change the top and bottom margins as well, you must use one of the other methods.

 PROCEDURE

To change your margins in the Document dialog box, choose Format ➤ Document and type the desired settings in the Right, Left, Top, and Bottom text boxes. Then click OK.

 NOTE

This method is arguably the most "professional" way to change margins, because you can specify exact settings. In addition, you have several useful options in this dialog box.

▲ The drop-down menus beside the Top and Bottom settings control whether pages are completely filled vertically. Choosing Exactly instructs Word to stretch the text to the exact top and bottom margins. Selecting At Least ensures that your margin will be no smaller than the setting, although it might be larger.

▲ If you know that your file is going to be printed and bound as a two-sided document, click the Mirror Even/Odd option. This sets the right and left margins for right-hand (*recto*) pages as mirror images of

117

those for left-hand (*verso*) pages, calling them *Inside* and *Outside*. The inside margin is the left margin for a recto page and the right margin for a verso page.

▲ A *gutter margin* is a strip along the margin that you leave blank for binding purposes. On single-sided documents, this is the left margin; on double-sided, the inside margin. This command is really superfluous, though, because you can simply make the left or inside margin bigger to accommodate the binding space.

PROCEDURE

To change your margins in Print Preview, choose File ➤ Print Preview (⌘-Option-I) and grab one of the margin handles (your mouse pointer will turn into a cross).

Crosshair cursor

Then drag the margin lines to the desired position, as shown in Figure III.10. Your position will be shown at the top of the Print Preview screen.

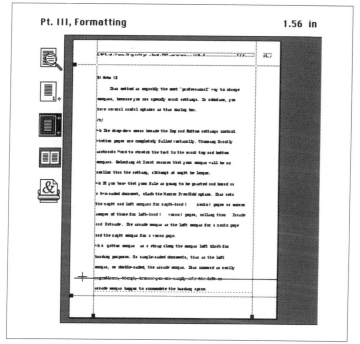

Figure III.10: Drag a margin box to adjust the margins

  NOTE

This method can be useful if you want to see exactly where pages will break. Print Preview does not allow you to make adjustments as exact as those you can make using the Document dialog box, however, and you cannot set gutters or specify mirrored margins.

SEE ALSO

Indenting

Part VI, Print Preview

COLUMNS—THE TRICK TO GREAT NEWSLETTERS ▲

People often use word processors these days to make newsletters. With its new frame column features, Word 5 is well suited to this task.

The shorter a line of text, the easier it is to read. This is especially true for small type sizes. While you wouldn't want to format a report as two or three columns, in-house and public newsletters look really snazzy when they are laid out this way.

PROCEDURE

To format a section as two or three columns, select the text and click on one of the column buttons in the ribbon.

NOTE

If you feel that the columns are too close together, or if you decide you want more than three columns, you can specify these settings in the Section dialog box.

 PROCEDURE

To specify other column settings, choose Format ➤ Section and type your settings in the Number and Spacing text boxes.

┌─Columns─────────────────
│ **Number:**　┌─────────────┐
│ 　　　　　　│ 4 　　　　　│
│ 　　　　　　└─────────────┘
│ **Spacing:**　┌─────────────┐
│ 　　　　　　│ 0.5 in 　　　│
│ 　　　　　　└─────────────┘
└─────────────────────────

FORMATTING

121

SNAPGUIDE TO PROFESSIONAL FORMATTING ▲

Like most other sophisticated tools, Word 5 produces the best results when in the hands of the creative professional. But that shouldn't discourage you. You don't need to be a professional typesetter to get a professional look to your documents. Word 5 allows you to do actual page layout, even if you know nothing about typesetting.

Whether you are looking to live up to the expectations of today's business world, or hope to excel at low-level desktop publishing, this SnapGuide will give you some pointers on professionally formatting a document. As you are reading through this section, keep in mind the golden rule of layout design: *Don't annoy the reader with the layout.* A good layout should not distract attention from the content.

Emphasis

Word offers you some half-dozen character enhancements. Only three of them, though, have a place in serious business documents: boldface, italics, and (occasionally) small caps.

Professional typesetters prefer italics to underlining as a means of emphasizing text. In this book, for example, you'll notice that emphasis is effected through italics. Underlining is really a holdover from typewriter days, when it was your only option.

You will see boldface in this book, too. The distinction between the uses of boldface and italics is blurry, but boldface is usually used with recurring elements (the first line in Procedure heads, for instance), while italics are used to emphasize unrelated bits of text (first use of terms, words used as words, and so on).

Small caps can be an effective alternative to words that are already in all capitals (such as product names and acronyms).

If you follow the above guidelines, you won't go wrong. Feel free to experiment, though, and to break the rules every once in awhile. You might find, for instance, that a certain type of heading really stands out nicely when it has a double underline.

Choosing a Font

While Word groups fonts and font sizes with character enhancements, you must consider the effect of typeface at the page layout level. Readers usually see paragraphs as visual elements, not as a bunch of words. Thus, there are three things to decide upon when choosing a font: proportionality, serif, and point size.

Proportionality refers to the amount of horizontal space each letter takes up. In a *monospace* font, each letter takes up the same amount of space. (Courier and Monaco are monospace fonts.) The overall feel of monospace is stodginess: it looks like typewritten text. Avoid mono-space fonts, unless you are trying to give the impression of a computer printout or typewritten material. *Proportional* fonts are those where each letter takes up a different amount of space. (Times, Palatino, Bookman, Helvetica, and Avant Garde are proportional fonts.) These give a "typeset" look to your text, and are easier to read.

Serifs are the picks or tails on fonts—fonts that have "feet" (such as Times, Palatino, and Zapf Chancery) are called serif fonts. Fonts that lack feet (such as Helvetica and Avant Garde) are called *sans serif* fonts—"without serifs." Traditionally, serif fonts are used for body text while sans serif fonts are reserved for headings, captions, and isolated bits of text. The rationale is that the serifs help guide the eye over the page, and so are appropriate for normal, body text. Sans serifs, though harder to read, are eye-catching, so they are well suited to headings.

Point size refers to the actual height of the font you're using. Body text is usually 10 to 12 pts, while headings start at 12 pts and go from there. Two things to keep in mind with point size are leading and readability. The *leading* is the vertical spacing between lines. The leading within a paragraph should be at least 1 pt greater than the point size of the font. For instance, a 12-pt font should have 13-pt leading. Readability is a qualitative term: don't use a font that's so small your readers will have trouble reading it.

 NOTE

As for the font itself, you must use your best judgment. Palatino gives a weighty, official look; Times gives a brisk, "newsy" look; Bookman is a large, very legible font; Helvetica is narrow and elegant; Avant Garde is rounded and modern looking; and Zapf Chancery is a fancy script font. You must determine the tone you wish to convey and then choose a font to match it.

Page Layout

Here are a few general guidelines:

- ▲ Avoid cluttering your pages. Give the layout room to "breath."

- ▲ Do not use more than two fonts on a page; if you do decide to use several, it's preferable to choose very different looking fonts.

- ▲ For dense text, consider running your document in a two- or three-column format.

- ▲ For a more "official" feel, justify your paragraphs both right and left. Conversely, for a more informal look, make your paragraphs ragged right (left-justified).

- ▲ Use lots of leading, both within and between paragraphs, when you can get away with it.

- ▲ Avoid using more than three major graphic elements per page (these might include a large header, a drawing, and a rule).

ENHANCING
YOUR WORK WITH WORD 5's
SPECIAL FEATURES

___

If you've read this book from the beginning, you've already learned 90 percent of what you need to know to make professional looking documents. Parts IV, V, and VI go into more depth. Here in Part IV, we'll take a close look at some of Word 5's "goodies"—features that aren't required for good looking documents but that can really jazz them up or save you time.

HEADERS AND FOOTERS ▲

In any document, there are elements that you'll want to have on every page. The most obvious are page numbers: you number your pages so people can easily locate what they're looking for. Other elements that you might want to repeat on every page are the title of the document, the author, or the date. Adding such material is very easy in Word.

PROCEDURE

To add a header to every page, follow these steps:

1. Go into Normal view and choose View ➤ Header. A header window will appear.

2. Type the repeating text, as shown in Figure IV.1, formatting it as you would any other text. Optionally, click one of the "field icons" at the top of the header window (see *Inserting a Field Code* below).

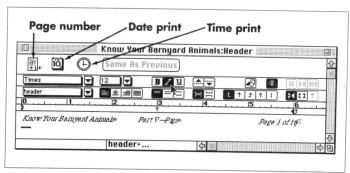

Figure IV.1: A header window—notice Word's preset tabs (one center and one right)

3. Close the window.

Whatever you've typed will appear at the top of every document page. To view headers in place, go into Page Layout view or Print Preview.

NOTE

The techniques for setting up and manipulating footers are identical to those for headers, except you choose View ➤ Footer instead of View ➤ Header. Headers and footers are section-specific commands: you can have different headers and footers in a document if you break it into sections. If you do so, though, be sure to click in the proper section before creating or editing a header or footer.

Inserting a Field Code

The three icons at the top of the header window are shortcuts for adding page-number, date-print, and time-print *fields*.

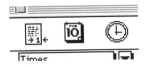

No actual text is added with fields; rather, a code is inserted that essentially tells Word "print today's date," "print the page number," etc. A field is surrounded by a dotted box.

Page 1 of 1

In this case, the page number will change for each page automatically.

Changing the Position of a Header or Footer

By default, Word positions your header ½" from the top of the page (footers ½" from the bottom of the page). But you can easily adjust this setting to place a header or footer anywhere you like.

 PROCEDURE

To change the position of a header, choose Format ➤ Section to reach the Section dialog box and adjust the settings in the From Top and From Bottom text boxes in the Header/Footer area.

 NOTE

You can have a special header or footer (or nothing at all) on the first page of your document. Click the Different First Page option in the Section dialog box before closing it. Two new commands will appear on the View menu: First Header and First Footer. They work the same

ENHANCING

as regular headers and footers, except that what you type
will appear on the first page only.

SEE ALSO

Part VI, Page Numbers

FOOTNOTES ▲

This is a feature most typists would kill for. You may have
bits of information that you do not want to mention in
the regular flow of text, such as sources, cross-references,
and asides. Often, the best way to handle them is as *footnotes.* These are entries at the bottom of the page that are
referenced by numbers in the running text. What makes
Word's footnoting function so terrific is that it is automatic. The program determines where the footnote
should start, how much room it will take up, and what its
number should be. It even adds a thin rule to separate
the footnote from the running text.

PROCEDURE

To add a footnote, follow these steps:

1. Go into Normal view, place the cursor where you
   want the reference mark, and choose Insert ➤
   Footnote. A dialog box will come up. You can
   specify a particular symbol (such as an asterisk or
   dagger) for the reference mark or you can accept

the default, a number that increases by increments of 1. Make your choice and click OK.

2. Word will insert the reference mark in the text

kept pigs w.

cies.[1]   Tec]

r ten weeks

and open a footnote pane at the bottom of the screen.

3. Type the text of the footnote (the cursor will have jumped into the footnote pane).

---

[1]Lowenstein, R. and Blumenfeld, H., "A Controlled Study in Porcine Aptitude," The Wisconsin Journal, Sept. 1992.|

4. You can either close the pane or leave it open. Closing it gives you more of the screen to work with. To close the footnote pane, double-click the split box.

When you print the document, all footnotes will automatically print at the bottom of the pages on which they're referenced, with a rule to separate them from the body text, as shown in Figure IV.2.

<u>PART V: PIGS</u>

As anyone who has kept pigs will tell you, they are one of the most intelligent of the domesticated food species.[1] Technically, the term *pigs* is incorrect. Pigs are actually hogs that are under ten weeks old. Once past that age, they are no longer pigs. For most people, what they know about pigs is what they learned by following the adventures of Wilbur in the classic children's story, *Charlotte's Web*.[2]

---

[1]Lowenstein, R. and Blumenfeld, H., "A Controlled Study in Porcine
Aptitude," The Wisconsin Journal, Sept. 1992.
[2]White, E.B., *Charlotte's Web*, Harcourt, Brace, and Jovanovich, 1945.

Figure IV.2: How footnotes look when they're printed

KEYBOARD SHORTCUT

⌘-E is the shortcut for inserting a footnote.

NOTE

To add more footnotes, just follow the steps given above. Word will automatically use the correct number. You can even insert a new footnote prior to ones you've already added. Word will automatically renumber the others. Conversely, if you delete a footnote, Word will renumber all footnotes that followed it. To delete a footnote, delete its reference in the text.

 PROCEDURE

To see all footnotes in your document, choose View ➤ Footnotes. Word will split your window, opening a footnote pane at the bottom. The shortcut for this command is ⌘-Shift-Option-S.

 PROCEDURE

To change the position of your footnotes, choose Format ➤ Document and choose one of the options from the Position drop-down menu.

You also have the option of restarting your footnotes on each page or section, or of starting them with a number other than 1.

 SEE ALSO

Part III, Dividing a Document into Sections

YOU AS THE ARTIST ▲

The *picture window,* a new Word 5 feature, just might help you unleash your artistic potential. The picture window is a drawing utility within Word that allows you to create simple line art for your documents. While a complete discussion of how to use this feature is beyond the scope of this book, Figure IV.3 gives some idea of what you can do.

 PROCEDURE

To use the drawing window to create a graphic, follow these steps:

1. Choose Insert ➤ Picture or click the picture icon on the ribbon.

   The picture window will open, as shown in Figure IV.3. (If you have used the menu command, an Open dialog box will appear; click New Picture to reach the picture window.)

2. Use the tools to be creative—enjoy yourself and have some fun!

3. When you are finished, close the picture window. Your drawing will be inserted at the cursor.

The inside back cover of this book lists all the tools you'll find in the drawing window.

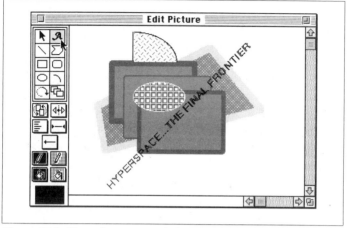

Figure IV.3: Exercise your artistic talents in the picture window

NOTE

Graphics you create in the drawing window are *embedded* in your document (see the *SnapGuide* to *Part IV* for more on embedding). This means you can easily edit pictures by double-clicking on them. The drawing window will come up with your graphic ready to be revised.

CREATING AND USING FRAMES

One of Word 5's most significant advances is the *frame*. A frame is a container for text or graphics. Unlike the usual delimiters (margins, indents, etc.), frames can be moved freely about the page. You can even place them in the middle of other text, which will flow around them automatically, as shown in Figure IV.4. (Frames replace Word 4's Position command.) Applications for frames include pull-quotes (a few lines of text set in large type, often boxed), graphics, charts, and tables—all of which can be placed in the middle of the running text.

The initial size of a frame depends upon the size of the highlighted material. If you've framed a line of text, the width of the frame will be the length of the line. If you want a different width (say, only a few inches), though, you must resize the frame with the Frame dialog box.

 PROCEDURE

To create a frame, follow these steps:

1. Highlight the text, graphics, or other objects that you want to frame.

2. Choose Insert ➤ Frame. Word will change to the Print Preview window, placing the highlighted material in a frame, which appears to you as a box.

Enhancing Your Work with Word 5's Special Features

PART V: PIGS

As anyone who has kept pigs will tell you, they are one of the most intelligent of the domesticated food species.[1] Technically, the term *pigs* is incorrect. Pigs are actually hogs that are under ten weeks old. Once past that age, they are no longer pigs. For most people, what they know about pigs is what they learned by following the adventures of Wilbur in the classic children's story, *Charlotte's Web*.[2]

Contrary to popular belief, pigs are very clean animals. Expressions such as *filthy as a pig* and *smells like a pig* stem from their propensity to bath in mud. Their predilection for filth is not a matter of choice, though. This function is critical to their survival, because, unlike humans, pigs cannot sweat. They loll in the mud to keep from overheating.

Recently, it has been all the rage, among yuppies at any rate, to keep miniature pot-bellied pigs as house pets. They are very clean animals, are essentially born house-broken, and make loyal and friendly companions. Even miniature pigs grow quite large, though, so pigs are certainly not ideal substitutes for Cocker Spaniels as lap dogs.

Recent research conducted by Rollie Lowenstein and Hector Blumenfeld, of the University of Wisconsin and Edward Fraud of the Marine Biological Laboratories in Woods Hole, Massachusetts suggests that people take a liking to pigs more readily than to other domesticated food species, such as cows and sheep, because, as Dr. Fraud states, "There's something of the pig in all of us. I mean, who can honestly say that at one time or another, he hasn't run around on all fours, grunting and squealing, and rolled in the mud. I know I have."

And then, of course, there's pork.

> *"...who can honestly say that at one time or another, he hasn't run around on all fours squealing..."*
>
> *—Dr. E. Fraud*

[1] Lowenstein, R. and Blumenfeld, H., "A Controlled Study in Porcine Aptitude," The Wisconsin Journal, Sept. 1992.
[2] White, E.B., *Charlotte's Web*, Harcourt, Brace, and Jovanovich, 1945.

ENHANCING

Figure IV.4: Text flows around frames and their contents

3. To reposition the frame on the page, move the mouse pointer into the frame. The pointer will turn into a cross. Click and drag the frame to where you would like it to go. It may take a moment to redraw the screen, so be patient. When you're finished, close the Print Preview window.

 NOTE

When you return to Normal view after creating a frame, the framed material will still be in the same place in the flow of text. Never fear: this is merely one of the idiosyncrasies of Normal view. If you click the show/hide ¶ button in the ribbon, you'll notice that Word places a small black square next to framed material. This indicates there is special formatting.

> *"...who can honestly say that at one time or another, he hasn't run around on all fours squealing..."*
>
> *—Dr. E. Fraud*

You can see frames in place in either Print Preview or Page Layout view.

PROCEDURE

To resize a frame, follow these steps:

1. Highlight the frame you wish to resize.

2. Choose Format ➤ Frame. The Frame dialog box will appear.

3. Adjust the settings in the Frame Width box.

Frame Width: `3 in` ▼

From Text: `0.13 in`

   Notice also the From Text box. You can specify here how far Word should keep body text from the frame.

4. Click OK. When you return to Print Preview, you will find the frame is now the size you've specified. You may have to play with text a bit to get the right look.

NOTE

You *cannot* resize a frame by changing its indents or the page margins. This changes the arrangement of the text, but not the size of the frame. Changing the size or length of the text will alter the height of the frame, but not its width.

PROCEDURE

To reposition a frame, go into Print Preview. The frame will appear as a box, just as when you first created it. Click and drag the box anywhere on the page to reposition the frame. Finally, click the Close box.

 NOTE

While you can place a frame either partially or entirely in the margins, try not to push a frame too close to the edge of the page. Most laser printers don't print right to the edge of the page; if you have elements that run to the edge, chances are they'll be *cropped* (cut off).

 PROCEDURE

To unframe framed material, highlight the material, choose Format ➤ Frame, and click Unframe and OK. (It can be difficult to get rid of a frame by just deleting its contents.)

 SEE ALSO

Part II, Word's Three Views

Part VI, Print Preview

Part VI, Marginalia

SYMBOLS MADE EASY

One significant edge Word for the Mac has over PC word processors (including Word for Windows) is the ease with which you can insert special symbols. PC word processors require you to remember arcane ASCII codes to insert things as basic as em-dashes and round bullets. Not so with Word for the Mac. In Word 5, this already simple procedure is even easier.

 PROCEDURE

To insert a special symbol, choose Insert ➤ Symbol, click the desired symbol, and close the Symbol window. Your selected symbol will appear at the cursor. You can insert as many symbols as you like before closing the window.

 KEYBOARD SHORTCUT

When you click a symbol in the Symbol dialog box, its keyboard shortcut (if it has one) will appear in the box at the bottom of the window, along with the ASCII code.

```
‡ · ‚ „ ‰ Â Ê Á Ë È Í
♣ Ò Ú Û Ù ı ^ ~ ¯ ˘ ˙
decimal:247: Option+Shift+n
```

EQUATION EDITOR ▲

Here's a new feature that will be a boon to engineers, mathematicians, and other scientists. *Equation Editor,* like the drawing window, is a utility that comes with Word. Unlike the drawing window, though, Equation Editor is a separate program: it can run completely independent of Word.

In fact, if you are not running under System 7, you'll have to use Equation Editor separately, then paste your equations into Word via the Clipboard. Under System 7, though, equations you create in Equation Editor can be embedded in any Microsoft program.

A thorough description of Equation Editor is beyond the scope of this reference, but the *User's Guide* to the program is well written and lucid. Following are some general usage guidelines.

 PROCEDURE

To create equations with Equation Editor, follow these steps:

1. Choose Insert ➤ Object.

2. Double-click on Equation in the Object Type list. Equation Editor will start up.

3. Create your equation, as shown in Figure IV.5.

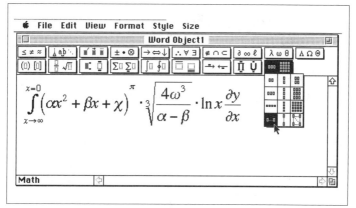

Figure IV.5: Equation Editor

4. Close Equation Editor, and your equation will appear at the cursor.

NOTE

Since equations are *embedded objects* (see the *SnapGuide* to *Part IV* for more on embedding), you can easily revise them. Simply double-click on an equation and Equation Editor will reappear, with your equation ready for editing.

Equation Editor is not always the best way to create formulas, especially if they are not complicated. Word also has a large collection of formula typesetting commands. These are far too numerous to list here, but a complete list appears in the SYBEX book *The Mac Book of Microsoft Word,* by Ron Mansfield.

BORDERS FOR IMPRESSIVE EFFECTS ▲

One easy way to spruce up ordinary documents is by including borders. A *border* is simply a line running along one of the sides of your text. You can have borders on all four sides if you want. For example, the frame in Figure IV.4 is completely surrounded by borders. In this case, the frame is said to be *boxed*. Borders work on the paragraph level, but you can surround several paragraphs with one continuous border. Let's take a look at Word 5's new, simplified method of adding borders.

 PROCEDURE

To add borders, follow these steps:

1. Select the paragraph or paragraphs you want to add borders to.

2. Choose Format ➤ Border. The Border dialog box will appear, as shown in Figure IV.6.

3. Click on one of the sides of the page graphic to add a border. Click the Box icon to add borders to all four sides.

4. Specify any other options you wish, as explained here:

   From Text adjusts the distance from the border to the text or graphics it surrounds (in points).

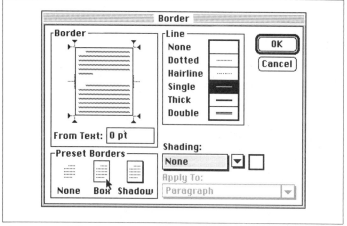

Figure IV.6: The Border dialog box

Line controls the properties of the border itself. If you've specified multiple-sided borders, you must choose the border you wish to affect before changing its properties.

Shadow adds a *drop-shadow* behind the border. This effect gives the impression of *relief* (three-dimensionality).

Shading provides various levels of backscreen behind the selected paragraphs. Note that you do not need to have a border to have a screen.

5. Click OK.

NOTE

Here's a neat trick. While Word has no provision for *reversed-out* text (white text on a black background), you can use the border feature to achieve this effect. Select the text you want to change, choose Format ➤ Character, and change the Color to White. Click OK to leave the Character dialog box. Then, with the text still selected, choose Format ➤ Border and set the Shading to 100%. If you find yourself doing this often, you may wish to create a style for it, calling it Reversed Out or some such.

PROCEDURE

To remove a border, follow these steps:

1. Highlight the appropriate paragraphs.

2. Choose Format ➤ Border.

3. Click on None in the Preset Borders box.

4. Click OK.

SEE ALSO

Part III, Character Styles

SETTING UP TABLES

A *table* is a grid of rows and columns. Where each column meets each row, they make *cells*. By entering text or other material into the cells, you can give the material a relational context. (Spreadsheets are really just large, special-function tables.) Having introduced tables in Word 4 to popular acclaim, Microsoft has concentrated its efforts in Word 5 on ironing out the bugs and making the feature more intuitive. Certainly, the menu commands that govern a table's size and constitution are intelligently laid out, and the ruler's table scale button provides a lot of flexibility.

 PROCEDURE

To insert a new table, choose Insert ➤ Table, specify the number of rows and columns you want, and click OK. Word determines the column widths automatically, based on the number of columns and your page margins. Clicking Format inserts and selects a table and brings up the Table Cells dialog box, discussed next.

 PROCEDURE

To change the look of a table, follow these steps:

1. Select the table you want to change.

2. Choose Format ➤ Table Cells; the Table Cells dialog box will pop up, as shown in Figure IV.7.

3. Adjust the settings, as explained here, to achieve the look you want. Click Apply to see the effect of each change.

ENHANCING

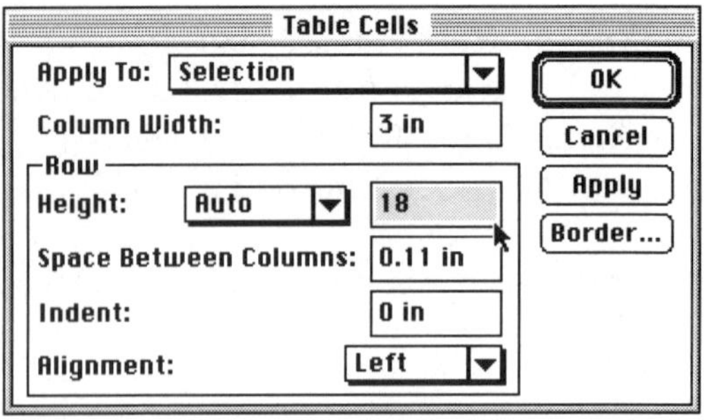

Figure IV.7: The Table Cells dialog box

Apply To tells Word whether to apply your settings to selected cells or to the whole table.

Column Width determines the width of your columns.

Height determines the vertical height of your rows. Note that you can click in the text box and type in an exact height (in points), or use Auto or At Least.

Space Between Columns leaves a small amount of space between the columns themselves. This prevents column text from running together, and keeps borders away from text should you choose to add them.

Indent moves entire rows by actually changing your indent. This usually pushes your table into the margin, so use with caution.

Alignment governs the *page* alignment of the entire table, *not* the *cell* alignment of the individual cell's contents.

4. Click OK to put your changes into effect. Clicking Border brings up the Border dialog box, discussed in the section on borders.

 NOTE

You can also use the ruler's table scale button to adjust the size of table columns. To do so, click on the table scale button on the right side of the ruler.

Notice that, instead of tabs, you now see little *T*s in the ruler. Each *T* controls the position of a column's edge. To resize a column and change the width of the table, just drag any of the *T*s. To resize columns without changing the size of the table, hold down Shift while dragging a *T*. It is usually best to select a whole table before adjusting column width.

 PROCEDURE

To add or remove rows and columns from a table, follow these steps:

1. Select the rows or columns you want to delete. (If you want to add rows or columns, select the same number that you want to add. For example, to add two columns, begin by selecting two columns.)

ENHANCING

2. Choose Format ➤ Table Layout. The Table Layout dialog box will appear.

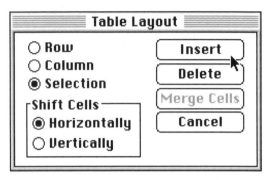

3. Specify whether you want to affect rows, columns, or just the selected cells, and click Insert or Delete. You can also indicate which way Word should shift the affected rows or columns.

 KEYBOARD SHORTCUT

To add a new row to an existing table, place the cursor in the bottom-rightmost cell and press Tab.

 PROCEDURE

To change existing text into a table, select the text you wish to convert, choose Insert ➤ Text to Table, and click OK. In the Convert From box, you can specify

how Word should break the text into table cells. The best
candidates for this are columns of information separated
by tabs.

  PROCEDURE

To edit text and move around in tables, follow these
steps:

▲ To move from one cell to the next (left to right),
press Tab.

▲ To actually tab over within a cell, you must press
Option-Tab.

▲ Each cell has, on the left-hand side, a selection bar
similar to a document selection bar. Clicking in it
selects the entire cell. (When you are in a cell's
selection bar, the mouse pointer turns into a right-
pointing arrow.)

▲ To select an entire row, double-click in the *document* selection bar next to the row.

▲ To select an entire column, slide the mouse
pointer to the top of the column until it turns into
a down-pointing arrow,

and click. Alternatively, hold down Option; the
mouse pointer will turn into the down-pointing
arrow, and a click will select the whole column.
Double-click the arrow to select the whole table.

ENHANCING

▲ To select an entire document from within a table, hold down ⌘ and click in any cell's selection bar.

NOTE

Tables are not always the best solution for arranging tabular material. Experience will teach you when tabs, columns, or even other programs are more expedient, but here are some guidelines:

▲ For snaking, newspaper-column arrangements of text, use Word's column feature.

▲ For short bits of information that don't run over within their columns, use tabs.

▲ If you want to use leaders of any kind, use tabs.

▲ If you have large blocks of text, especially ones that run over within their columns, use tables.

▲ For applications where you want to perform a lot of calculations or include intertabular cross-referencing, you'd probably be better off using a spreadsheet program, such as Excel.

SEE ALSO

Part III, Tabbing

Part III, Columns

Borders for Impressive Effects

INSERTING JUST ABOUT ANYTHING ▲

Among the many improvements of Word 5 over Word 4 is the new Insert menu. If you look at Word 4, you'll see that the Insert menu was much narrower in scope. Now it encompasses section breaks, voice annotations, symbols, frames, entire files, and objects, among others. (Inserting objects is discussed in detail in the *SnapGuide* to *Part IV.*)

 PROCEDURE

To insert an item into a document, place the cursor where you want the inserted item to fall and choose the item you wish to insert from the Insert menu. One of three things will happen:

▲ The item (such as a page or section break) will be inserted.

▲ A dialog box will appear, asking you to confirm settings; clicking OK inserts the item.

▲ You will be prompted by a dialog box to choose a file (for files, pictures, and objects), which will then be inserted.

 SEE ALSO

Part III, Page Breaks

Part III, Using the Glossary

ENHANCING

TABLES OF CONTENTS (TOCs) ▲

A *table of contents* (TOC) is a list of major headings in a document. Usually you place a TOC at the beginning of a document—along with the pages on which the headings can be found—to help readers find the information they need. Creating a TOC is a two-step process: first you create or specify the TOC entries, then you compile the TOC. By default, Word places a TOC at the beginning of a document. You can move it anywhere you like, though.

Creating TOC Entries

You can specify TOC entries in one of two ways. If you have used Word's default heading styles for the headings in your document, you don't need to do anything: the default heading styles are automatically treated as TOC entries. If you've used your own styles for your headings, though, you must code each TOC entry. These methods are exclusive.

PROCEDURE

To apply a standard Word style to a heading, highlight the heading and choose Format ➤ Style. Click on the All Styles option if the list shows only document styles, and then double-click on the appropriate head level (they are called *heading 1, heading 2,* etc.).

PROCEDURE

To specify a head as a TOC entry, highlight the heading in question, and choose Insert ➤ TOC Entry. A TOC *code* will appear in front of the entry. A semicolon will appear after the entry unless it's followed by a paragraph mark (¶).

.c.PART V: PIGS

This code tells Word to include the heading when it compiles a TOC. Like other Word codes, the TOC code is dynamic.

 NOTE

TOC codes are automatically formatted as *hidden text* (you can tell by the dotted underline); whether you can see the code depends upon whether you can view hidden text. To display or hide hidden text, choose Tools ➤ Preferences, click the View icon, and either activate or deactivate the Hidden Text option in the Show box. The code is formatted as hidden so that it won't print out on your drafts; you can manually insert TOC codes just by typing *.c.,* but if you do so, you may wish to format them as hidden text (⌘-Shift-V).

Compiling a TOC

Identifying your TOC entries is really the hard part. Compiling a TOC is easy.

 PROCEDURE

To compile a TOC, follow these steps:

1. Choose Insert ➤ Table of Contents. The Table of Contents dialog box will appear, as shown in Figure IV.8.

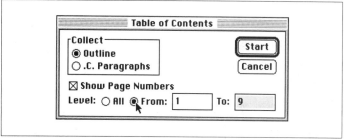

Figure IV.8: The Table of Contents dialog box

2. Specify whether you want Word to work from your headings (you must have used Word's standard heading styles for this to work)—including the head levels it should use—or from codes. Also, you can exclude page numbers if you wish.

3. Click Start. In a few moments, Word will compile the TOC and place it at the beginning of your document. If it is a long document, this can take awhile.

SEE ALSO

Part III, Creating and Using Styles

INDEXING ▲

An *index* is a list of concepts or key words in a document, along with the pages on which the words can be found, that helps readers find information quickly. Usually you place an index at the end of a document. Creating an

ENHANCING

index is a two-step process: first you specify the index entries, then you compile the index. By default, Word places an index at the end of a document. You can move it anywhere you like, though.

Specifying Index Entries

Unfortunately, there is no style shortcut to index entries: you must actually code each entry. In addition, you can specify index subentries (words that are considered subordinate to other words).

 PROCEDURE

To specify a word as an index entry, highlight the word, and choose Insert ➤ Index Entry. An index *code* will appear in front of the entry,

has kept .i.pigs; will tell you, they

and a semicolon after it. This code tells Word to include the word when it compiles an index. Like other Word codes, the index code is dynamic.

 PROCEDURE

To specify a word as an index subentry, highlight the word and choose Insert ➤ Index Entry. An index code will appear in front of the entry. Place the cursor between the index code and the word and type the main entry and a colon.

who has kept .i.hogs:pigs; will tell

When you compile the index, the word will appear as a subentry under the specified main entry.

hogs 27
   pigs 27

Alternatively, you can work from a compiled index. Highlight the desired entry and choose Format ➤ Style. Then double-click on the level of index entry you wish to apply.

 NOTE

Index codes are automatically formatted as *hidden text*; see the Note on TOCs for more information. You can manually insert index codes by typing *.i.* before the word and a semicolon after, but if you do so, you may wish to format them as hidden text (⌘-**Shift-V**). **Warning:** Be sure you don't select the space after a word when specifying it as an index entry; otherwise, the space will be included when Word compiles the index.

Compiling an Index

Coding your index entries is really the hard part. Compiling an index is easy.

PROCEDURE

To compile an index, follow these steps:

1. Choose Insert ➤ Index. The Index dialog box will appear, as shown in Figure IV.9.

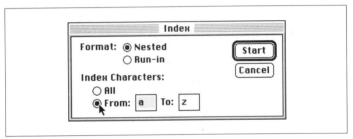

Figure IV.9: The Index dialog box

2. Specify whether you want Word to indent sub-entries below main entries (Nested) or include them on the same line as main entries (Run-in). You can also limit the range of entries by changing the letters in the Index Characters From and To boxes. You might want to do this if your document is very long. Split the alphabet and compile each part separately so Word doesn't run out of memory.

3. Click Start. In a few moments, Word will compile the index and place it at the end of your document. If it is a long document, this can take awhile.

VOICE ANNOTATIONS

An *annotation* is a comment, suggestion, or criticism that an editor or reviewer adds to a document. You don't normally annotate your own documents. A *voice* annotation is one that is added as a recorded message. This nifty new Word 5 feature is probably better honored in the breach than in the observance, but it's still worth knowing about.

 NOTE

You must have a Mac-compatible recording device to record voice annotations. You can playback voice annotations from any Mac, though.

 PROCEDURE

To record a voice annotation, follow these steps:

1. Place the cursor where you wish the annotation to appear.

2. Choose Insert ➤ Voice Annotation. The Voice Record dialog box will appear.

ENHANCING

3. Click Record and begin speaking into your recording device. Monitor the Level (volume) box and try to keep it from turning completely black. Click Pause to suspend the recording; click Pause a second time to resume recording. Click Stop when you are finished. Be sure to finish your annotation before the circle turns entirely black.

4. Click OK. Word will insert a voice annotation icon (formatted as hidden text) at the cursor.

ten weeks old. Once past

 NOTE

As you can see, Voice Annotations take up quite a bit of disk space. A five-second recording at Best Quality takes up 115K. You can use annotation space more effectively by changing the quality from Best to either Better or Good. The same recording that took up 115K at Best Quality took up only 22K at Good Quality.

 PROCEDURE

To playback voice annotations, follow these steps:

1. Choose View ➤ Voice Annotations or double-click on any voice annotation icons. The Voice Annotations dialog box will appear.

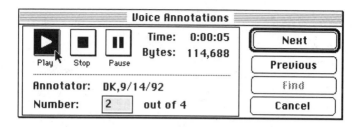

2. Click Play to hear the annotation. Click Pause to suspend playback and Stop to cancel it altogether.

3. Click Next or Previous to reach other voice annotations in your document, and then click Play to hear them.

NOTE

To delete a voice annotation, simply delete its icon.

SNAPGUIDE TO OBJECT LINKING IN WORD 5 ▲

Word 5 offers several features to help you keep information in documents current. These features do so through dynamic connections: when you change a document, all others connected to it can be updated to reflect the changes. The three features are *publish and subscribe, link,* and *embed.* All require System 7.

While the logistics of these three features are fairly straightforward, there is a lot of confusion about which one to use for a given situation. Therefore, the emphasis in this SnapGuide will be on suitability rather than on usage (although procedures and hints will be given, too).

Publishing and Subscribing

Publish and subscribe (Apple Edition Manager) involves three files to achieve a link. A portion of the source file (the *publisher*) is saved under a new file (the *edition*). Then other documents (*subscribers*) can grab the information in the edition file for their own use. The advantage, of course, is that any changes to the publisher can be automatically echoed in the subscribers.

Publish and subscribe is probably the best of the three data-exchange features for work groups connected by a network, since you don't need any other application apart from the one you're subscribing with. Furthermore, you can decide whether to update the information in the subscribers—it is not necessarily automatic.

 PROCEDURE

To publish a portion of text or other material, follow these steps:

1. Highlight the material you wish to publish.

2. Choose Edit ➤ Create Publisher. The Publish dialog box will appear.

3. Give the file a relevant name.

4. Click Publish.

The material will be stored as an edition file on disk.

 PROCEDURE

To subscribe to an edition file, choose Edit ➤ Subscribe To. The Subscribe dialog box will appear. Locate the desired edition file and double-click its name. The material will appear in your document at the cursor.

 NOTE

To cancel a subscription, select the subscriber material, choose Edit ➤ Subscriber Options, and click on Cancel Subscriber. For updating to work properly, any changes

to the publisher document must be saved before any subscribers are updated.

Linking

Linking (*dynamic data exchange* or *DDE*) involves two documents: a *source* and a *destination*. Linking is actually easier
than publishing and subscribing, because there is no middle file. To create a link, you copy material from the
source file and use Paste Special to paste it into the destination file. Once again, you can automatically update
any changes to the source file.

Linking is probably best used to link disparate parts
of a single document, or material from several different applications. You cannot link from one machine
to another; all applications you use must be on your
machine.

 PROCEDURE

To create a link between two documents, follow these
steps:

1. Copy the material you want to link from the *source*
   document (Edit ➤ Copy or ⌘-C).

2. Position the cursor in the *destination* document
   where you want the material to appear.

3. Choose Edit ➤ Paste Special. The Paste Special
   dialog box will appear.

4. Click on Paste Link. The material will be pasted into the destination document.

 NOTE

To cancel a link, select the linked material, choose Edit ➤ Link Options, and click on Cancel Link.

Embedding

Embedding objects in Word is the easiest of the data-exchange methods, inasmuch as it uses only one file and all updates are automatic. It is probably best for documents that incorporate information created in other applications (spreadsheets, graphics, equations, etc.). The advantage is that the object is placed in your document in toto, with all of its application attributes. This means if you copy the document to a floppy and then open that floppy on another Macintosh, you can edit the object, provided the Mac has the original application the object was created in. You cannot embed over a network.

 PROCEDURE

To embed an object, just choose Insert ➤ Object and double-click on the desired object type. The requisite application will open, allowing you to create or assemble the object. When you are finished, choose File ➤ Update (⌘-Q).

PART

V

PROOFING:
THE FINISHING TOUCHES

———

Word 5 offers you six postediting, or *proofing*, tools to help you check your documents for common errors and improve your writing. While these features are collectively called proofing tools, you can actually use them at any time when composing documents.

Do not underestimate the power of these features; a computer monitor is not easy to read and this reduces the chances that you'll see any errors you might make. Merely using the spell checker can save you a great deal of embarrassment. As we explore each proofing tool, try to decide how you could use them most efficiently.

SPELL CHECKING ▲
———

Simply put, a *spell checker* examines your document to make sure all the words you've used are legitimate. Word 5's spelling utility is one of the most advanced and intuitive electronic spell checkers I've seen. It is extraordinarily good at guessing what you intended to type, even when you are using recondite or technical words.

A spell checker works by trying to match every word in a file against a *dictionary* (a list of accepted spellings). If it cannot find a match, it highlights the word and flags it as unfamiliar. By default, Word's spell checker uses a standard dictionary called U.S. English Dictionary. You can also instruct Word to use dictionaries you've created that contain special terms. See *Part VII, Creating Custom Dictionaries.*

Note that the spell checker cannot check words for *context.* For example, it wouldn't flag the sentence *Though it was raining, he decided to go for a wok,* though you clearly intended to use *walk.* This is because Word's spell checker has no function beyond confirming that *wok* is a correctly spelled word in English.

PROCEDURE

To use the spell checker, follow these steps:

1. Highlight the text you want to check; if you want to scan an entire document, make sure nothing is selected.

2. Choose Tools ➤ Spelling. Word will begin to check your document, moving toward the end. Word won't *appear* to be doing anything until it runs across an unfamiliar word (if there are no unfamiliar words, skip to step 4). At this point, the Spelling dialog box will appear, as shown in Figure V.1.

3. Word is quite adept at guessing what you were trying to type. Often it will provide the correct spelling in the Change To box. Click the Change

PROOFING

```
┌─────────────────────────────────────────────────────────┐
│  ┌───────────────────────────────────────────────────┐  │
│  │▫▫▫▫▫▫▫▫▫▫▫▫▫▫▫▫▫▫▫▫▫▫ Spelling ▫▫▫▫▫▫▫▫▫▫▫▫▫▫▫▫▫▫│  │
│  │  Not in Dictionary: primre                        │  │
│  │                                                   │  │
│  │  Change To:   ┌──────────────┐  ┌─────────┐ ┌───────────┐│
│  │               │ primer       │  │ Ignore  │ │ Ignore All││
│  │  Suggestions: ┌──────────────┐  └─────────┘ └───────────┘│
│  │               │ primer     ⬆│  ┌─────────┐ ┌───────────┐│
│  │               │ primmer     │  │ Change  │ │ Change All││
│  │               │ premiere    │  └─────────┘ └───────────┘│
│  │               │ première   ⬇│  ┌─────────┐ ┌───────────┐│
│  │               └──────────────┘  │  Add    │ │  Close    ││
│  │  Add Words To: │Custom Dictionary▼│ │Suggest│ │Options...││
│  └───────────────────────────────────────────────────┘  │
└─────────────────────────────────────────────────────────┘
```

Figure V.1: The Spelling dialog box

button to correct the misspelling, or click Ignore if you do not want to change the spelling.

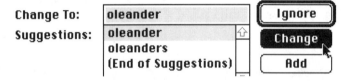

If you know you have made the same mistake later on, click Change All, and Word will correct similar occurrences without prompting you. To change the flagged word to one of the other words in the Suggestions list, double-click on the desired word. To leave the unfamiliar word alone, click Ignore; if it occurs later in the document and you don't want to be prompted each time, click Ignore All. If Word cannot find any words that resemble the unfamiliar word, it displays the message "No Suggestions," which means you're on your own. Go grab your favorite dictionary if you're not certain you've spelled the word right. Finally, if the checker finds a repeated word, it will offer you the choice of deleting it. The other options are explained in *Part VII, Creating Custom Dictionaries.*

4. When Word reaches the end of your document, one of three things will happen:

▲ If you began your spell check from the beginning of the document, you will see a message box letting you know the spell check has concluded. Click OK.

▲ If you started in the midst of the text, you will be asked if you wish to continue the spell check from the beginning of the document. Click OK to continue or Cancel to end the check.

▲ If you selected a word or passage, Word will inform you that it has validated the passage and give you the opportunity to check the rest of the document. Click OK to end the check or Continue Checking to check the rest of your text.

5. It is a very good habit to save your document after spell-checking it. To do so, choose File ➤ Save (⌘-S).

KEYBOARD SHORTCUT

The keyboard shortcut for the spell checker is ⌘-L.

SEE ALSO

Grammar Checking

Part VII, Spelling

GRAMMAR CHECKING ▲

New to Word 5 is the *grammar checker*. Similar to the spell checker, the grammar utility scans your document for common grammar and syntax errors.

NOTE

Unfortunately, the grammar checker requires *huge* amounts of RAM. In fact, you cannot run the grammar checker practically on less than 4 Mb of RAM, and it would be wise to increase the allotted RAM for Word before running grammar checks. I found that, for a 7000-character document, the grammar checker actually exhausts the default allotted memory (1024K).

PROCEDURE

To increase Word's allotted memory, follow these steps:

1. Quit Word (⌘-Q) and return to the Finder.

2. Locate Word itself, using File ➤ Find (⌘-F) if necessary.

3. Select the program's icon and choose File ➤ Get Info (⌘-I).

4. Type in a new Current Size in the Memory box.

The higher you set the allotted memory, the faster Word will run.

5. Close the Get Info box and restart Word.

PROCEDURE

To run a grammar check, follow these steps:

1. Highlight the sentence you want to check; if you want to scan an entire document, be sure nothing is selected.

2. Choose Tools ➤ Grammar. Word will begin to check your document, moving toward the end, scanning until it runs across a grammar infraction. At this point, the Grammar dialog box will appear, as shown in Figure V.2.

3. If Word can correct the potential error, it will offer alternatives in the Suggestions box. Click Change to accept the highlighted suggestion. You can preview how a sentence will read before making a change by sliding the mouse pointer into the Suggestions box. It will become a pointing hand. Click

PROOFING

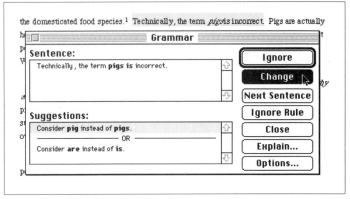

Figure V.2: The Grammar dialog box

once in the Suggestions box to see how the revised
sentence would read, as shown in the Sentence box.

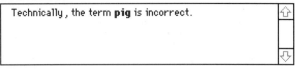

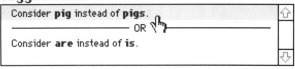

If Word cannot find any alternatives, it displays the
message "No Suggestions" or "No correction available." Occasionally, Word will express quaint disap-
probation with such statements as *It is preferable to
avoid beginning a sentence with **And*** or *This appears to
be a run-on sentence*, leaving it up to you to fix the

problem. If you are not sure what a rule means, click Explain and Word will try to clarify it for you. To leave the flagged sentence alone, click Ignore; if the same issue arises later in the document and you don't want to be prompted each time, click Ignore Rule. To ignore the rest of the sentence, click Next Sentence. Finally, if the checker finds a misspelled word, it will open the Spelling dialog box, discussed in the section *Spell Checking*.

4. When Word reaches the end of your document, one of three things will happen, as detailed in the *Spell Checking* section.

5. It is a good habit to save your document after a grammar check. To do so, choose File ➤ Save (⌘-S).

KEYBOARD SHORTCUT

The keyboard shortcut for the spell checker is ⌘-**Shift-G**.

NOTE

You can customize the grammar utility to provide the best level of review for your documents. You do this in the Grammar category of the Preferences dialog box. See *Part VII, Grammar*.

PROOFING

THE THESAURUS IS NOT EXTINCT!

▲

Perhaps my personal favorite new feature in Word 5, the *thesaurus* is a veritable cornucopia of quintessential rhetoric. More simply, it is a dictionary of synonyms and antonyms. You will often find yourself repeating words when you write; the thesaurus can offer alternate words that convey the same meaning but that spice up your prose with a little variety.

 PROCEDURE

To use the thesaurus, follow these steps:

1. Place the cursor in or next to the word or phrase you want to find a synonym or antonym for.

2. Choose Tools ➤ Thesaurus. The Thesaurus dialog box will appear, as shown in Figure V.3.

3. Word will offer suggestions in the Synonyms box. To substitute one of them for the highlighted word, click on the desired word (which appears in the With box) and then click Replace. If the word has several meanings or can be more than one part of speech (for example, *fish* can be a noun or a verb), there will be definitions in the Meanings For box. Click the most appropriate definition. If Word knows any antonyms (words of the opposite meaning) for the highlighted word, *Antonyms* will

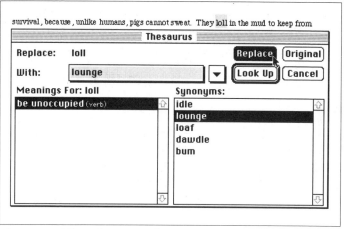

survival, because, unlike humans, pigs cannot sweat. They loll in the mud to keep from

Thesaurus

Replace: loll

With: lounge

Replace | Original

Look Up | Cancel

Meanings For: loll

be unoccupied (verb)

Synonyms:

idle
lounge
loaf
dawdle
bum

Figure V.3: The Thesaurus dialog box

    appear in the Meanings For box. Click on *An-tonyms* to see Word's suggestions.

4. Unlike the grammar and spell checkers, the thesaurus vanishes after performing its duty, without any prompting.

 NOTE

    You can keep looking up synonyms for each successive word you select in the Synonyms box. For example, if you were to click Look Up instead of Replace in Figure V.3, you would then see a list of synonyms for *lounge.* Since this can lead you quite astray from your original term, Word offers you two ways to retrace your steps. To get back to the original word, click Original and then click Look Up. To get back to one of the penultimate words,

PROOFING

click on the arrow next to the With box, and a list will
drop down showing all the words you've looked up.

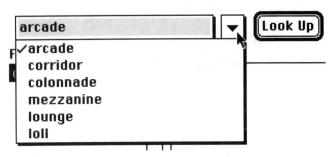

  SEE ALSO

Part VII, Thesaurus and Hyphenation

HYPHENS AND DASHES ▲

Okay, I admit hyphens aren't the most interesting thing
in the world. But the hyphen *is* a tool of writing. Dashes,
which are sometimes created using the hyphen key, are
often confused with hyphens. There are three types of
hyphens and two kinds of dashes:

▲ The *normal* or *hard hyphen* is the most common of
the hyphens, found in hyphenated words and
phrases such as *black-and-white, world-beater,* and *run-
of-the-mill.* When you hit the hyphen key on your

keyboard, hard hyphens are what you get. They always print, too, no matter where the word or phrase falls on the line.

▲ By contrast, *optional* or *soft hyphens* print only when the hyphen falls at the end of a line. Word inserts soft hyphens when you do an automatic hyphenation, as discussed in the section *Automatic Hyphenating*. Soft and hard hyphens are identical in length.

▲ The rarest hyphen of all is the *nonbreaking hyphen.* There are some hyphenated words that would look odd if they were broken over a line (such as in *catch-22* or telephone numbers). It's best to use nonbreaking hyphens for these words: no matter where the word falls in the line, it will not be broken.

▲ *En dashes* are slightly longer than hyphens and much more rare. The only common use for the en dash is to separate numerical quantities, as in expressions such as *pages 44–51* and *9:30–11:00.*

▲ The big brother of the en dash is the *em dash.* These are usually at least twice as long as a hyphen. They are used to indicate a full break in the flow of a sentence. This book features them fairly regularly—can you spot any? Using a real em dash (as opposed to two hyphens in a row) makes a document look a lot more professional.

PROCEDURE

To insert a special dash, choose Insert ➤ Symbol and click on the dash you want to insert.

decimal:208: Option+ -

To insert a special hyphen, you must use the keyboard shortcut listed below.

 KEYBOARD SHORTCUT

The keyboard shortcuts for en and em dashes are **Option-hyphen** and **Option-Shift-hyphen**. The keyboard shortcuts for nonbreaking and soft hyphens are ⌘~ and ⌘-hyphen.

NOTE

If soft hyphens don't fall at the end of a line, the only way to see them is to click the show/hide ¶ button in the ribbon or to choose View ➤ Hide ¶ (⌘-J).

Automatic Hyphenating

As you are finishing up a document, one of the last things to consider doing is a hyphenation pass. If your paragraphs are formatted as double-justified, intelligent use of hyphens can reduce unwanted space within lines. If the paragraphs are left-aligned, hyphens can even outline breaks. The narrower the columns of text, the more important this becomes.

Consider, as an example, the paragraph shown in Figure V.4.

> As anyone who has kept pigs will tell you, they are one of the most intelligent of the domesticated food species.[1] Technically, the term *pigs* is incorrect. Pigs are actually hogs that are under ten weeks old. Once past that age, they are no longer pigs. For most people, what they know about pigs is what they learned by following the adventures of Wilbur in the classic children's story, *Charlotte's Web*.[2]

Figure V.4: A paragraph before hyphenation

The paragraph has been formatted to be justified along both margins, leaving unsightly gaps between the words (*loose lines*) and a *widow* (a single word on a line). Let's do an auto-hyphenation to see if we can fix it.

PROCEDURE

To run an automatic hyphenation, follow these steps:

1. Select the paragraph or paragraphs you want to hyphenate; if you want to scan your whole document, be sure nothing is selected.

2. Choose Tools ➤ Hyphenation. The Hyphenation dialog box will appear.

3. If you want Word to hyphenate the document without verification, click Hyphenate All. (You can specify whether Word should hyphenate capitalized words by clicking on Hyphenate Capitalized Words.) Otherwise, click the Start Hyphenation button. Word will hum along until it finds a candidate for hyphenation. It will show the word in the Hyphenate box, allowing you to reposition the hyphen if you wish, as shown in Figure V.5. To do so, click within the word where you want the hyphen to fall.

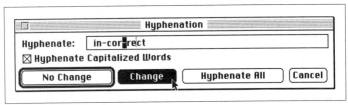

Figure V.5: The Hyphenation dialog box

4. To ignore the word, click No Change; to insert the hyphen, click Change.

5. When you reach the end of the document, Word will either ask if you want to keep scanning from the beginning or will inform you that it has concluded its hyphenation pass. In our example, if we agree to Word's one suggestion (hyphenating *incorrect*), the paragraph is significantly tightened, and the widow is *run up* to the previous line (see Figure V.6).

> As anyone who has kept pigs will tell you, they are one of the most intelligent of the domesticated food species.[1] Technically, the term *pig* is incorrect. Pigs are actually hogs that are under ten weeks old. Once past that age, they are no longer pigs. For most people, what they know about pigs is what they learned by following the adventures of Wilbur in the classic children's story, *Charlotte's Web*.[2]

Figure V.6: The paragraph after hyphenation

NOTE

By default, Word inserts soft hyphens during automatic hyphenation. This way, if you later revise the text, words that no longer fall at the ends of lines will not be hyphenated.

SEE ALSO

Part VII, Thesaurus and Hyphenation

MEASURING YOUR WORDS

Unless you have a special need to know the *exact* length of your document in terms of words or lines, the *word count* feature is little more than a diversion. However, if you write for a magazine that sets a word limit on articles, or if you want to determine a document's character count before sending it over a modem, this feature can be very useful. It certainly couldn't be easier to use.

PROCEDURE

To run a word count, choose Tools ➤ Word Count. The Word Count dialog box will appear.

	Main Text	Footnotes	Total
☒ **Characters**	15277	0	15277
☒ **Words**			
☒ **Lines**			
☒ **Paragraphs**			

[Count] [Cancel]

Select the units you wish to count (characters, words, lines, and paragraphs) and click Count.

HOW TO BE CALCULATING

It can be very handy to quickly add up columns of numbers or to perform basic math without having to access the Calculator under the Apple menu. Word provides a simple calculating feature for just such occasions.

By default, the Calculate command sums (adds together) any numbers you highlight. You can also have it perform other simple calculations by using the proper operator, as shown here:

To...	*Use*...
Add	+
Subtract	–
Multiply	*
Divide	/
Figure a percentage	%

 PROCEDURE

To perform a calculation, select the numbers in question

and choose Tools ➤ Calculate. Word will show the answer in the status area (in the lower-left portion of the Word document window)

138

and place it in the Clipboard; if you would like to insert the answer in your document, place the cursor where you want it to go and choose Edit ➤ Paste (⌘-V).

PROOFING

KEYBOARD SHORTCUT

The keyboard shortcut for calculate is ⌘-=.

NOTE

If you plan to do a lot of intertabular calculations, you'd probably be better off using a spreadsheet program, such as Excel.

SNAPGUIDE TO PROOFING ▲

While Word's many proofing tools can help you polish a document, there is no substitute for checking it over yourself. If at all possible, this check should be done with a hardcopy of your work. Problems such as redundancy, inconsistency, and non sequiturs are often hidden by a word processor's scrolling screens.

Not to downplay Word's powerful proofing utilities, but you might wish to think of them as being supplementary to your own editorial inspection. In this SnapGuide, we will take a look at some strategies for using Word's proofing tools effectively and consider some guidelines for checking your hardcopy.

Strategies for Using Word's Proofing Tools

When you are actually composing a document, you will probably find yourself using only two of the proofing commands regularly: Calculate and Thesaurus. The others are best used after you finish writing.

Tools ➤ Calculate

As explained in the section *How to Be Calculating*, the calculation tool can perform simple math. Consider using it as you work if you are presenting simple figures. You can *never* verify your numbers too often.

Tools ➤ Thesaurus

As described in the section *The Thesaurus Is Not Extinct*, the thesaurus is a great way to avoid word repetition and add a little variety to your writing. It can serve a more meaningful, more general purpose, though: It can give you a different perspective on your words.

When you write, you often have a firm idea of what you wish to say. Actually hitting upon the words that will most precisely convey your meaning, though, is very, very difficult. What you write will be interpreted in different ways, depending upon the reader. Choosing your words with care can narrow the range of possible misinterpretations.

Let's look at a practical example.

In the second sentence of the paragraph above, I had originally written

> ...actually *choosing* the words that will most *accurately* convey your meaning...

Realizing that *accurately* wasn't exact enough, I used the thesaurus to come up with *precisely*, which conveys my meaning unambiguously. Later on, after writing the last sentence of the paragraph, I noticed I had used a form of *choose* twice. The second usage conveyed exactly what I wanted to say, so I decided to replace the first. The thesaurus didn't offer any synonyms that had the right connotation of considered thought, though, so I substituted a more casual phrase myself. This illustrates a good lesson: always consider the shades of meaning that words convey. Merely substituting synonyms at random will make your writing sound dilettantish.

The Other Tools

The spell checker, grammar checker, and hyphenation tools are very easy to use, as explained in their respective sections in *Part V.* They should be used in that order, too. You might even want to save hyphenating until after you have completed your own editorial pass and made your changes to a document.

Guidelines for Your Editorial Pass

Besides correcting redundancies and inconsistencies, you can smooth out the logical flow of your writing when proofing hardcopy. Again, let's look at a practical example.

This paragraph was the chapter introduction to a section on composition called *How to Write a Dun Letter*, which we cut on the advice of our lawyers:

> Using Word, you have its powerful features at your fingertips. More powerful than any other word processor, these are the same features that make Word ideal for composing dun letters, memos, academic and business reports, articles and papers, and more.

The paragraph suffers from several problems: there is repetition of the words *features* and *powerful;* the second sentence is confusing; it's unclear what the features mentioned in the second sentence are; and finally, the paragraph doesn't really sound like a chapter introduction.

What I did to fix the paragraph was to isolate the main ideas in a list:

1. With Word, you have many powerful features at your fingertips.

2. Word is more powerful than other word processors.

3. Word's features (spell checker, thesaurus, search and replace, etc.) make it ideal for writing and editing.

4. You can use Word to write dun letters, memos, academic and business reports, articles, papers, and more.

Sorting out the main ideas made it a lot easier to rewrite the paragraph. All I did was link them together logically, replace a few words to avoid redundancy, and add an introductory phrase. The paragraph as it ended up was:

> In this chapter, we will explore Word's composition tools, which are more powerful than those of other word processors. These features (spell checker, thesaurus, search and replace, etc.) make Word ideal for writing dun letters, memos, reports, articles, and papers.

Of course, proofing is rarely as simple as I'm making it sound. But you might want to think of it as just another aspect of writing—which it is, in many respects. Learning to edit is a worthwhile investment of time and effort, because it will ultimately make you a better writer.

PART

VI

PRINTING
YOUR DOCUMENTS

———

Word's default print settings are adequate for most business needs; however, you can gain greater control of many aspects of your printed hardcopy. In fact, the more sophisticated your documents become, the more you will probably find yourself tinkering with margins and page setups to get exactly the right look. The print quality of your documents is important—after all, most of the time, it is through your hardcopy that you communicate with others.

BASIC PRINTING ▲

———

You can get good printouts without any tinkering, simply by using Word's File ➤ Print command. It brings up the Print dialog box, shown in Figure VI.1, where you can choose from a number of printing options. (This figure shows the Print dialog box for a LaserWriter.) All options are discussed here except page ranges, which are covered in the section *Printing Page Ranges*.

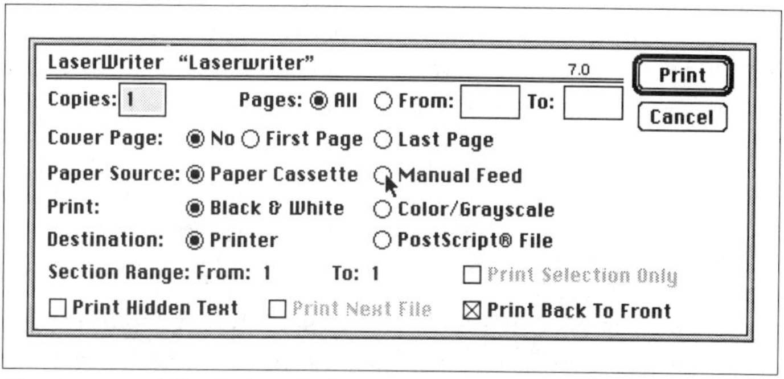

Figure VI.1: The Print dialog box for a LaserWriter

Copies specifies the number of copies Word should print.

Cover Page tells Word whether to print a special page before each print job listing the name of the document, the time and date of printing, and the number of pages, along with other information. This option is useful if people send a lot of jobs to one printer; otherwise, deactivate this feature and save a few trees.

Paper Source informs your printer whether to take sheets from its paper tray or to wait for you to feed the paper manually.

Print instructs your printer to print black-and-white hardcopy or colors and grayscales. If you're using a LaserWriter, you can fool it into printing shades of gray by using colors in your Word document and selecting the Color/Grayscale option (see *Part III, Creating and Using Styles*).

Destination governs whether your file is printed to a printer or to an Encapsulated PostScript (EPS) file. The latter option is useful when you want to have copy of a document on disk with all of its PostScript printing information. Usually you cannot print files directly to typesetting machines; rather, you must send EPS files.

Section Range allows you to specify a particular section or group of sections to print, provided that such divisions exist in your document. Along with page range, this is another command that can save trees!

 PROCEDURE

To print a document, bring up the Print dialog box in one of the following ways:

▲ Choose File ➤ Print.

▲ Press ⌘-**P.**

▲ In Print Preview, click the print icon.

Once you have reached the box, specify any desired options and click Print.

NOTE

There are four options in the Print dialog box.

▲ **Print Hidden Text** tells your printer to print text formatted as hidden in your document. (It must actually be showing for this to work properly—see *Margins and Hidden Text.*)

▲ With **Print Next File**, you can tell Word the next file to print in a specified series. See *Page Numbers.*

▲ **Print Selection Only** allows you to print just the highlighted portion of text.

▲ **Print Back To Front** instructs printers to print the last page first and the first page last. If your printer prints out pages print-side up, however, selecting this option will cause your pages to come out in front-to-back order.

HIDDEN TEXT ▲

The term "hidden text" is a bit misleading; often you can see hidden text quite clearly! Generally it means text that does not print by default, though you can *specify* that hidden text be printed (see *Printer Options*). What is important to realize about hidden text is that it can cause discrepancies between what you see on-screen and what you get on your printed output.

PRINTING

For example, if you have a lot of hidden text on a page, and you have activated the Show Hidden Text option in the Preferences dialog box, you will see the hidden text on-screen. Furthermore, Word will treat the hidden text just like any other; a line with hidden text will break if the hidden text pushes it far enough. Figure VI.2 illustrates just such a page. The hidden text (which includes index entries and an annotation) has dotted underlining.

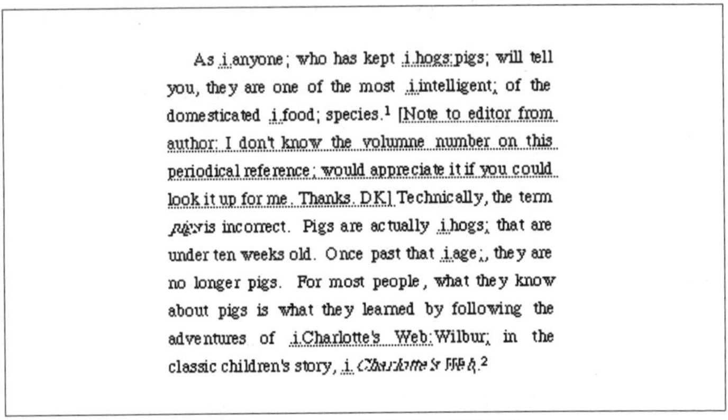

As ¡anyone¡ who has kept ¡hogs¡pigs¡ will tell you, they are one of the most ¡intelligent¡ of the domesticated ¡food¡ species.[1] [Note to editor from author: I don't know the volume number on this periodical reference¡ would appreciate it if you could look it up for me. Thanks. DK] Technically, the term ¡pig¡is incorrect. Pigs are actually ¡hogs¡ that are under ten weeks old. Once past that ¡age¡, they are no longer pigs. For most people, what they know about pigs is what they learned by following the adventures of ¡Charlotte's Web¡Wilbur¡ in the classic children's story, ¡ *Charlotte's Web*¡.[2]

Figure VI.2: A paragraph chock-full of hidden text

When you *print* this paragraph, however, the line breaks will be completely different, and any hyphenation you've added will no longer be applicable (see Figure VI.3). In longer text, there might also be confusion as to where pages break. This can be a disaster if you create an index or table of contents (TOC) with hidden text showing, because the pages that items print on might differ from the page numbers given in the index or TOC. The way to get around all this is to simply turn off the Show Hidden Text option.

> As anyone who has kept pigs will tell you, they
> are one of the most intelligent of the domesticated
> food species.[1] Technically, the term *pigs* is incor-
> rect. Pigs are actually hogs that are under ten weeks
> old. Once past that age, they are no longer pigs. For
> most people, what they know about pigs is what they
> learned by following the adventures of Wilbur in the
> classic children's story, *Charlotte's Web*.[2]

Figure VI.3: The printed text has quite different line breaks

PROCEDURE

To hide hidden text, choose Tools ➤ Preferences, click
View, and turn off the Show Hidden Text option.

SEE ALSO

Part IV, Tables of Contents (TOCs)

Part IV, Indexing

OPTIMIZING YOUR PAGE SETUP

Before you begin a project, it's always a good idea to
determine what kind of a page setup you'll use, since
your choices can affect the format of your document. If
you intend to use 2.0" margins on all sides, for instance,
you'll probably want to avoid using a three-column

PRINTING

layout. You should look at your page setup before printing, as well, just to double-check that all the settings are
acceptable. If nothing else, this might save a few trees
that would otherwise be sacrificed to the god of er-
roneous printouts.

All of the settings we will discuss in this section are
found in the Page Setup dialog box, which you reach
by choosing File ➤ Page Setup (see Figure VI.4). The
decisions you make here will affect your entire document; there is no way to create individual printing instructions for different sections.

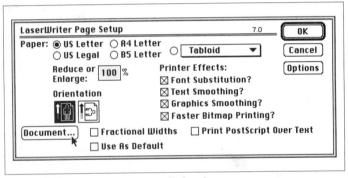

Figure VI.4: The Page Setup dialog box

  NOTE

Clicking the Document button in this dialog box takes
you to the Document dialog box, where you can specify
margins, position footnotes, and so on.

SEE ALSO

Part III, Moving Your Margins

Part IV, Footnotes

Size and Orientation

Depending upon your printer, you can have seven or more *page-size options* in Word 5, each of which you can print in either a *portrait* or *landscape orientation*. Portrait orientation is what most printers use automatically; it prints the text across the width of the paper. With land-scape orientation, the text is rotated 90°. If you are using a standard laser printer, this means you effectively have 14 page sizes to choose from, as catalogued in Table VI.1.

PROCEDURE

To change the paper size, choose File ➤ Page Setup, then click on the size you want in the Page Setup dialog box (US Letter is the default).

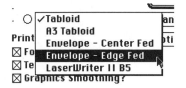

When you have made your choice, click OK.

Table VI.1: Word's Page-Size Options for a Standard Laserprinter

SIZE (PORTRAIT)*	WIDTH	HEIGHT
US Letter (default)	8½"	11"
US Legal	8½"	14"
A4 Letter (European standard)**	21 cm	29.7 cm
B5 Letter**	17.6 cm	25 cm
Tabloid	11"	17"
A3 Tabloid**	29.7 cm	42 cm
Envelope—Center Fed	4"	9½"
Envelope—Edge Fed	9½"	4"

*To calculate the landscape size, simply swap the height and width dimensions.

**These are international paper sizes.

PROCEDURE

To change the page orientation, choose File ➤ Page Setup, then click on either the portrait or landscape icon (portrait is the default).

Orientation

When you have made your choice, click OK.

NOTE

You can include custom paper sizes if you wish. See *Part VII, General* for the details.

Shrinking the Printout

You will occasionally find situations where you want your printout to be significantly smaller than usual. For example, you might be designing a small form, such as a borrowing slip for a library. Even though the finished form is to be small, you'll find it more convenient to work at a larger size when designing it (the text is easier to read, you can see all the punctuation, etc.). Then, you simply specify the percentage at which the text should be printed in the Page Setup dialog box, and Word will take care of printing the form at a smaller size. (This last step is best done early, as it affects many aspects of the final printout.)

PROCEDURE

To change the size of printed text, choose File ➤ Page Setup and specify a percentage in the Reduce or Enlarge text box (default is 100%).

Reduce or Enlarge: 75 %

When you are finished, click OK. When you print, the text will be sized to the percentage you have indicated.

Printer Effects

The distinction between *effects* and *options* is rather hazy, but since Word differentiates the two, we will too. With the LaserWriter, there are seven *printer effects* available to you in the Page Setup dialog box:

Font Substitution instructs your printer to replace any bitmap fonts you use in a document with similar LaserWriter fonts. This can end up looking awful, especially if you have a carefully designed format with precision text-spacing. (Selected by default.)

Text Smoothing smoothes out the edges of bitmap fonts. However, this can blur TrueType fonts. If you are using TrueType fonts, turn this option off. (Selected by default.)

Graphics Smoothing is similar to Text Smoothing, in that it smoothes the edges of bitmap graphics. Again, though, this can blur TrueType fonts. (Selected by default.)

Faster Bitmap Printing is useful if you are using mostly bitmap graphics. This option prints bitmap graphics faster by using more printer memory. (Selected by default.)

Fractional Widths improves the spacing of proportional fonts, simulating the spacing you see on-screen. Be careful when using this option, since it affects the look of your work on-screen, including line breaks and hyphenation. Consider using it during preparation of your document for final printout only.

Use As Default informs Word that it should use the specified paper size and orientation with every document. These settings will be applied to all new documents.

Print PostScript Over Text instructs Word to print regular text and graphics first and then PostScript graphics on top. You might want to do this to avoid having PostScript images covered up by text or other images.

 SEE ALSO

Part III, Using Fonts Effectively

Part V, Hyphens and Dashes

PRINTING

207

PROCEDURE

To select or deselect a printer effect, choose File ➤ Page Setup and click on the option. An *X* in its box means it's activated.

☒ Use As Default

Printing Options

If you are using a LaserWriter, you'll have six options from which to choose:

Flip Vertical turns the page upside down.

Flip Horizontal creates a mirror of the page when printing.

Invert Image creates a photo negative of the page (white on black instead of black on white). Handy for making plate negatives!

Precision Bitmap Alignment (4% reduction) reduces the size of the page to 96 percent to make up for the noninteger ratio between the resolution of your screen (72 dpi) and that of the printer (300 dpi).

Larger Print Area (Fewer Downloadable Fonts) frees up part of the memory usually reserved for storing downloadable fonts so you can have smaller page margins. Be aware, though, that with a laser printer there is a limit on how close you can print to the edge of a page.

Unlimited Downloadable Fonts in a Document frees up memory for fonts that must be downloaded to the printer. This means that the printer might have to download a font several times.

SEE ALSO

Part III, Using Fonts Effectively

PROCEDURE

To select or deselect a printer option, choose File ➤ Page Setup and click the Options button. The *printer* Options dialog box will appear, as shown in Figure VI.5. Click on any option to choose it; an *X* in its box means it's activated. When you click on an option, the image to the left will reflect your choice.

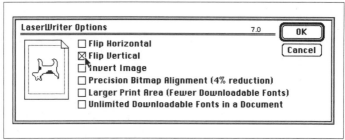

Figure VI.5: The *printer* Options dialog box

PRINTING

A KINDER, GENTLER PRINT MERGE ▲

The idea behind a *print merge* is fairly simple.

You have to mail a lot of copies of the same letter to different people and you want to address each one individually. You could make copies of the letter for each addressee and then type in each address. But the easier method is to use a print merge, in which you need just one copy of the letter (called the *main document*), with *merge fields* where the addressee information should go, and a second document (called the *data document*), with only the addresses. The print merge itself is the process of substituting each address into each merge field and printing each letter.

While print merges are straightforward in practice, actually pulling one off used to be quite difficult. Word 5, though, has a revamped print merge that is the soul of simplicity.

 PROCEDURE

To perform a print merge, follow these steps:

1. Create your main and data documents. See the section *The Print Merge Helper* below for details.

2. When you've prepared the two documents, choose File ➤ Print Merge. The Print Merge dialog box will appear.

3. Specify whether you want to print the documents directly to your printer or to a file on disk. The latter can be useful if you wish to edit or proof the letters before printing them. Also, this way you have disk records of the mailing.

4. Click OK.

NOTE

You can bypass the Print Merge dialog box by clicking on either the merge to printer icon

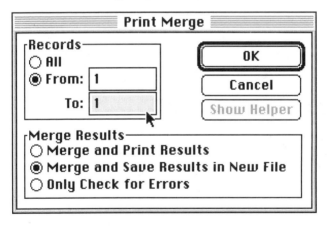

or the merge to file icon

in the print merge helper bar.

The Print Merge Helper

The main reason Word 5's print merge is so easy is the new *Print Merge Helper* feature. It essentially automates the tricky aspects of a print merge, leaving you to type in the information you want to include.

 PROCEDURE

To use the Print Merge Helper, follow these steps:

1. Create your main document. Do not insert your merge fields yet, though.

2. When you've written the main document, place the cursor at the very beginning (⌘-Home). Choose View ➤ Print Merge Helper. An Open dialog box will appear.

3. Click New and the Data Document Builder dialog box will appear.

4. Type in the names of the fields you want to add to your main document, clicking Add for each one.

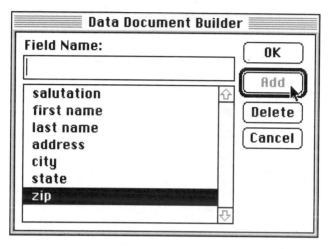

5. When you are finished, click Add and then OK. Word will open a new document and bring up the Save As dialog box.

6. Give the data file a name and click Save.

7. You will be returned to your main document. The print merge helper bar will appear beneath the ribbon and ruler. Also, Word will have added the name of your data document in a merge field right at the top of the main document.

«DATA MSW5 AY F (II):Part VI:Text Part VI:Examples:Dun Letter Names»Dewey, Cheetum & Howe

8. To insert the print merge fields, place the cursor where you'd like each field to go, then choose the correct field from the Insert Field Name dropdown list.

PRINTING

When you are finished, your main document should look something like Figure VI.6.

first name	last name	address 1	city	state	zip	salutation
Amy	Brice	1099 Spruce Street	Lubbock	TX	74636	Ms.
Joe	Shlabotnik	394 Elm Lane	Middletown	OH	48584	Mr.
Charlie	Chawelski	420 Main Street	Wellsboro	PA	32020	Chuck
Marv	Halitosis	544 Prison Way	Elmira	NY	29292	Birdie
Frankie	Frisch	32 BB Road	St. Louis	MO	44495	Lefty

Figure VI.6: A main document with merge fields

9. Return to the data document. The fields you have specified will appear in a table format.

10. Type in names and addresses for each individual you wish to send the letter to. You should end up with something like Figure VI.7.

«DATA MSW5 AYF (II):Part VI:Text Part VI:Examples:Dun Letter Names»Dewey, Cheetum & Howe

Attorneys at Law
738 Opcit Way • Los Angeles, CA 92383

7 April 1993

«first name»«last name»
«address 1»
«city», «state» «zip»

Dear «salutation»:

We know that you must be struggling to meet your tax deadlines. The fact is, we are, too. Which brings me rather quickly to the purpose of this letter. I have been advised by our accounting department that you are «weeks behind» weeks behind in your payments. Surely you can appreciate that if you retain the services of a reputable law firm such as DC & H, you have to pay through the nose for it. Pay through the nose...or bleed through it, as we like to say.

I needn't remind you that, in addition to signing over your firstborn child to us, you also agreed in your contract to the following clause:

> ...furthermore, if the party of the first part, heretofore known as Sucker, reneges in any way and for any reasons or causes, just or unjust, reasonable or unreasonable, legal or illegal, clear or...well, you get the idea, upon fees due and payable to the party of the second part, heretofore known as The Firm, he shall forfeit any or all of the protruding parts of his body, as seen fit by The Firm and its hirelings, specifically Joey No-Legs and Johnny Salami...

«salutation», I truly do not wish to have to instruct Joey and Johnny to pay you a visit, but please be assured that I will if we do not receive a check from you by the fifteenth. Oh, and don't try to leave the country; we'll be watching the airports.

Thank you in advance for your time, kind attention, and money.

Sincerely,

Andy Howe
President

PRINTING

Figure VI.7: A data document in table format

PRINT PREVIEW ▲

Print Preview is an uneditable bird's-eye view for checking the page layout of documents. It is always a good idea to use this feature before printing.

 PROCEDURE

To use Page Preview, choose File ➤ Print Preview. The Print Preview screen will appear. You can perform any of five functions:

▲ Zoom in on any portion of your document. Just click on the magnifying glass icon

and then click on the page where you want to zoom in. Microsoft removed this popular feature from Word 4, but has reinstated it in Word 5. Click the icon again to zoom out. (Double-clicking on the page accomplishes the same thing.)

▲ Add page numbers by clicking the page-number icon (see *Page Numbers*).

▲ Change the margins by dragging the margin lines (see *Part III, Moving Your Margins*).

▲ Switch back and forth from single-page view to two-page view by clicking on the page-display symbol.

▲ Print your document by clicking on the print icon (see *Basic Printing*).

KEYBOARD SHORTCUT

⌘-Option-I is the shortcut for reaching Print Preview.

PAGE NUMBERS ▲

Word offers you three ways of adding page numbers: from the Section dialog box, in a header or footer window, and in Print Preview. Be aware, though, that these methods are not exclusive. If you use all three, you'll end up with several sets of page numbers.

PROCEDURE

To add page numbers from the Section dialog box, choose Format ➤ Section and click Margin Page Numbers. If you want to, you can specify the position of the numbers by changing the settings in the From Top and From Right boxes. When you are finished, click OK.

PRINTING

NOTE

Word gives you five options for your page numbers, including Arabic, Roman numerals, and letters. Also, since page numbering is a section-specific command, you can restart the numbering of a new section at 1 by clicking the Restart at 1 option.

 PROCEDURE

To add page numbers in a header or footer window in Normal view, choose View ➤ Header (or Footer). When the header or footer window appears, click on the page number icon,

and Word will insert a page-number code. The great advantage of this method is that you can format the number and add text, such as *Page* n *of* whatever the total page count happens to be.

 PROCEDURE

To add page numbers in Print Preview, choose File ➤ Print Preview. When the Print Preview window appears, click on the page-number icon.

The cursor will turn into a **-1-**. Drag this to where you want to position the page number. You can tell where you are on the page by looking at the top of the Print Preview window (see the section *Print Preview*).

Creating and Numbering a File Series

There are many reasons to divide a single document into several different files. If you do this, though, you are faced with the problem of printing out the parts with sequential page numbering. The way around this dilemma is to use a *file series*.

PROCEDURE

To specify a file series, follow these steps:

1. Choose Format ➤ Document. The Document dialog box will appear.

2. Click File Series and the File Series dialog box will pop up.

PRINTING

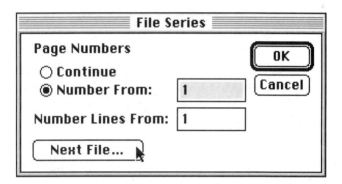

3. Here you can specify the starting page number for the file or click Continue. To specify the file that follows it, click Next File and choose the correct file from the list. Click Open and OK the other two dialog boxes.

Getting from Here to There with Go To

One of the many shortcuts Word offers for moving quickly around a document is *Go To*. This command simply takes you from your present position to a specified page.

PROCEDURE

To move to a specific page, choose Edit ➤ Go To and type the page number you wish to go to.

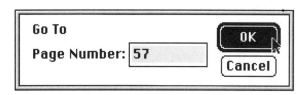

When you click OK, you will be taken to the top of the specified page.

KEYBOARD SHORTCUT

⌘-**G** is the shortcut for bringing up Go To.

NOTE

Double-clicking in the *page* section of the status area in the lower-left corner

Page 13

activates the Go To command. Also, you can go to a specific section of the document as well as a page. To do so, type *P* and the page number, then *S* and the section number. For example, to go to page 5 of section 2, you would type *P5S2*.

SEE ALSO

Part III, Dividing a Document into Sections

Printing Page Ranges

You will often find that you need to print only certain ranges of pages. You might have corrections on only a few pages of a draft or you might need only the first few pages of a report. At any rate, it saves trees to print only those pages you need. You specify page ranges when you print.

PROCEDURE

To specify a range of pages to print, follow these steps:

1. Choose File ➤ Print (⌘-P). The Print dialog box will appear, as shown back in Figure VI.1.

2. Move to the From box, and type the first page of the range.

3. Hit Tab to get to the To box, and type the last page of the range.

4. Click Print to print the range.

SNAPGUIDE TO PRINTING ▲

One of the most common dilemmas that arises with printing is fitting text on pages. We'll take a look at the topic in detail in this SnapGuide.

Fitting Text on Pages

Two problems with reports, brochures, and especially resumes are fitting your text comfortably on the page and making your page breaks look nice. Let's look at each of these separately.

 PROCEDURE

To fit all your text on one page, follow these suggestions:

1. First, take a look at your document in Print Preview. This will help you determine how much material you need to "pull back." If it is more than a half-page, you probably can skip step 2, since it won't be sufficient.

2. In many cases, simply adjusting your margins will rectify matters. See *Part III, Moving Your Margins* for full details, but the easiest way is just to click and drag your margins in Print Preview. Try repositioning the top and bottom margins before fiddling with the left and right ones, because the wider a text block is, the harder it is to read.

3. If pushing the margins out doesn't help, consider using a smaller typeface. You can even do this in 1-point increments; with TrueType fonts, you can size 12-point type down to 11 points and no one will be the wiser. It is best to avoid type sizes lower than 10 points, though. Also, be aware that some fonts take up a lot more room than others. Times and Helvetica, for instance, use line space much more efficiently than Bookman and Avant Garde.

4. If your document still stubbornly refuses to run back to one page, your only options are to revise the design to make it more space efficient, or to cut material. In the case of a resume, if you've got ½' margins all around with your text set in 10-point Times, you've probably got too much material on there anyway, and your resume will not suffer from a little trimming.

PROCEDURE

To make your pages break nicely, follow these steps:

1. Look at your document in Print Preview to determine where pages will break awkwardly (for example, leaving a heading alone at the bottom of a page). The best way to remedy problems like widows (lines by themselves) is to select them, choose Format ➤ Paragraph (⌘-M), and click the Keep With Next option. This ensures that no matter where the heading falls, it will be kept with the paragraph immediately following it. Similarly, if you don't want a paragraph or a set of paragraphs (cells in a table, for instance) to be separated, highlight them, choose Format ➤ Paragraph (⌘-M), and click the Keep With Next option.

2. If you still are getting bad breaks, and it looks like they are happening on every page, consider moving your document's margins. See *Part III, Moving Your Margins* for complete details, but the easiest way is just to click and drag your margins in Print Preview. If you had many bad breaks, this may remedy all of them. If not, go on to step 3.

3. If you have only a few bad breaks in your document, consider placing manual breaks. Insert manual breaks only when your document is *completely finished*, though; any revising you do subsequently might cause some very strange breaks, such as pages that print only two or three lines at the top. To insert a manual break, place the cursor where you want to end the page and choose Insert ➤ Page Break (Shift-Enter).

4. If you are a real stickler, you might want to look at some of the suggestions above for keeping text to one page; with judicious use, they can be applied to fix bad breaks as well.

PART

VII

CUSTOMIZING
WORD 5

In addition to the many terrific features discussed in other parts of this book, almost all aspects of Word can be personalized. You can change the appearance of the screen and menus to best suit your individual needs. What's more, Word allows you to save custom configurations in *settings files*—even if several co-workers share the same copy of Word, each can have his own personal configuration. This high level of flexibility is yet another example of the sensible planning that went into the design of Word.

WORD 5's DEFAULTS ▲

Before we get too enamored of Word's custom configurations, though, let's take a moment to consider the default, or "factory," settings. Most of these are quite reasonable and useful for many business applications. For example, the default margins (1" top and bottom, 1¼" left and right), line spacing (single, 12-point), and alignment (left-justified) are adequate for business correspondence and memos, school or business reports, and even scientific research papers. If you choose as your default font something like 12-point Times Roman, you'll be in like Flynn!

I strongly encourage you to fiddle around with the configuration, though, once you get comfortable with the program. If you're like most people, you'll probably find that a combination of custom and default settings works best (see the *SnapGuide* for this part for further tips and advice). Custom settings are controlled via two commands on the Tools menu: Preferences and Commands.

PREFERENCES ▲

The Tools ➤ Preferences command brings up a dialog box with the generic name of Preferences. You'll notice, though, as you click on each successive icon, that the look of the Preferences dialog box changes. Each of these icons is a different *category* of the Preferences dialog box, covering different aspects and features of Word. We will examine each category separately.

 PROCEDURE

To make changes in the Preferences dialog box, choose Tools ➤ Preferences. The dialog box will pop up, with the General category selected, as discussed next. Scroll until you see the category you want to work with, then click its icon. Make any changes in the category box. When you are finished, close the Preferences dialog box. Your changes will be saved to disk when you quit Word.

General

The General category appears automatically when you open the Preferences dialog box. If you are in another category, simply scroll until the General icon is in view

General

and click on it. The General category will appear, as shown in Figure VII.1.

Your Name:	Charlie Chawelski

Your Initials: CC

Custom Paper Size   Width:

Height:

Measurement Unit: Inch ▼

☐ "Smart" Quotes
☒ Background Repagination
☒ Include Formatted Text in Clipboard
☒ Drag-and-Drop Text Editing

Figure VII.1: The General category

Let's look at each of the options here.

> **Your Name** and **Your Initials** identify the user. Initially, these will note the name used when the program was installed. You can change them, however. The contents of these fields are used when you

insert an "author" entry from the glossary, to prefill the Summary Info box, and for voice annotations.

Custom Paper Size allows you to specify nonstandard paper sizes, which will show up in the Page Setup dialog box. Simply type in custom heights and widths, and they will appear in the Page Setup box as additional choices. (This will be dimmed unless your printer can accommodate unusual sizes.)

Measurement Unit identifies the default unit Word will use when you don't specify one in a text box. The "factory" setting is inches, but you can also choose centimeters, points, or picas.

"Smart" Quotes instructs Word to use fancy typesetter's quotation marks ("") in your documents. They work in pairs: the first one you type will look like a *66* (") and the second like a *99* (").

Background Repagination forces Word to periodically determine your document's page breaks. Leave this on unless you find that it slows your operations in Word or you have a specific reason you don't want your documents repaginated automatically.

Include Formatted Text in Clipboard determines whether text cut or copied to the Clipboard will have character and paragraph formats such as boldface, italics, double-spacing, right-alignment, etc. If this is unchecked, text will be cut or copied to the Clipboard as plain text.

CUSTOMIZING

Drag-and-Drop Editing enables or disables Word 5's new cut and paste operation that bypasses the Clipboard.

SEE ALSO

Part II, Drag-and-Drop Editing

Part III: Formatting for Great Results

Part VI, Size and Orientation

View

To reach the View category, simply scroll until you see the View icon

View

and click on it. The View category will appear, as shown in Figure VII.2.

Each box controls a different aspect of the physical appearance of Word on the screen. Let's look at the options you have here.

In the Show box, you have these four options:

Hidden Text shows any hidden text in your documents. It will not print, though, unless you click the Print Hidden Text option in the Page Setup dialog box.

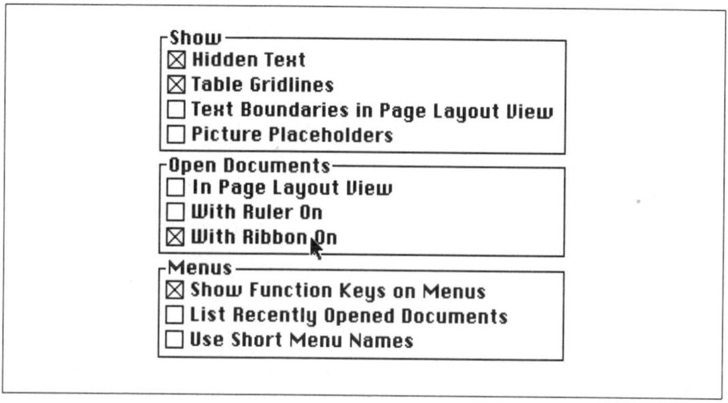

Figure VII.2: The View category

Table Gridlines shows dotted lines to delineate the rows and columns in tables. Don't confuse these with borders; unlike borders, gridlines will not print.

Text Boundaries in Page Layout View shows dotted lines in Page Layout view to mark the confines you have set for your text. These include margins, frames, headers and footers, and footnotes.

Picture Placeholders is a very useful feature if you have a slower Macintosh. When this option is enabled, Word will show gray squares or *placeholders* on-screen instead of graphics for any embedded elements, greatly speeding up scrolling.

In the Open Documents box, you have three options:

In Page Layout View opens all documents in Page Layout view.

With Ruler On opens all documents with the ruler showing.

CUSTOMIZING

With Ribbon On opens all documents with the ribbon showing.

In the Menus box, you have these three options:

Show Function Keys on Menus adds any default or custom function key shortcuts assigned to commands next to their names on menus. If you don't have an extended keyboard, you might want to disable this to unclutter your menus.

List Recently Opened Documents activates the new Word feature that appends near the bottom of the File menu the names of the last four documents opened. The advantage is that you can recall these documents simply by choosing one of the names. The disadvantage is that it is obvious what documents you've been working on.

Use Short Menu Names instructs Word to use abbreviated menu names.

File   Edit   View   Ins   Fmt   Font   Tools   Wnd   Work

This can be very practical if you have a small screen.

 SEE ALSO

Part II, Opening a File from Disk

Part II, The New Ribbon and Improved Ruler

Part II, Page Layout

Part IV, Setting Up Tables

Part VI, Hidden Text

Open And Save

To reach the Open And Save category, simply scroll until the Open And Save icon is in view

Open And Save

and click on it. The Open And Save category will appear, as shown in Figure VII.3.

☒ Always Interpret RTF
☐ Always Make Backup
☒ Allow Fast Saves
☒ Prompt for Summary Info
☒ Save Reminder Every ❘ 10 ❘ Minutes

Figure VII.3: The Open And Save category

Let's look at this dialog box's options.

Always Interpret RTF instructs Word to open files saved in Rich Text Format (RTF) without prompting you.

Always Make Backup tells Word to automatically create a backup file with the name *Backup of [file]*. This backup file will not have your changes saved to it, so

CUSTOMIZING

if you irreparably goof up, you can always return to your original. Note that Allow Fast Saves must be deselected for this to work properly.

Allow Fast Saves instructs Word to append changes to the end of the document on disk, rather than updating the whole document. While this is faster, it consumes a lot of disk space. Note that you must deselect Always Make Backup for this to work properly.

Prompt for Summary Info brings up a dialog box every time you save a new document. It's a very good idea to leave this on, as a reminder to fill in the summary info boxes. These can be invaluable when you are searching for a lost file.

Save Reminder Every *n* Minutes brings up a little dialog box reminding you to save your work. You can specify the interval.

SEE ALSO

Part II, Opening a File from Disk

Part II, Saving Your Work

Default Font

To reach the Default Font category, simply scroll until the Default Font icon is in view

Default Font

and click on it. The Default Font category will appear, as shown in Figure VII.4.

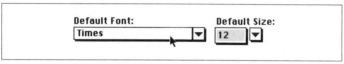

Figure VII.4: The Default Font category

  PROCEDURE

To change the default font or point size, click in either the Default Font or Default Size drop-down menus and select the new font or size. You can type nonstandard settings in the Default Size box. All new documents will open with the font and size you've specified as the default.

  SEE ALSO

Part III, Using Fonts Effectively

Spelling

To reach the Spelling category, simply scroll until the Spelling icon is in view

Spelling

and click on it. The Spelling category will appear, as shown in Figure VII.5.

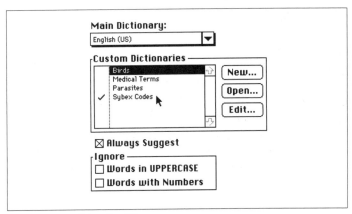

Figure VII.5: The Spelling category

You have four options:

The **Main Dictionary** drop-down menu offers choices other than English (US) only if you have purchased other main dictionaries from Microsoft or from third-party manufacturers.

The **Custom Dictionaries** drop-down menu gives you access to dictionaries you've created. These are discussed in detail in the section *Creating Custom Dictionaries* below.

Always Suggest instructs Word to suggest alternatives in the Spelling dialog box when it runs across an unfamiliar word.

In the **Ignore** box, you have two nonexclusive options: *Words in UPPERCASE* and *Words with Numbers*. The first is self-explanatory; the second ignores any words that have numbers in them, such as *R2D2, MI5, 10K,* and *70cm.*

Creating Custom Dictionaries

Word's Main Dictionary is extensive but not exhaustive. It's unlikely to recognize your name, or the names of your associates, business, or products. In addition, it is stumped by field-specific argot. That's where custom dictionaries come in.

A *custom dictionary* is a supplemental word list that the spell checker uses (if you tell it to) to match words. By creating a custom dictionary, you can create lists of words that are germane to your industry or field. For example, a parasitologist could add the name *Trypanosoma cruzi* to a custom dictionary and be assured that Word would never again consider it an unfamiliar term—unless, of course, it was actually misspelled.

The other nifty thing about custom dictionaries is that you can have as many as you like—if your profession is nursing and your avocation is ornithology, you can have

CUSTOMIZING

one custom dictionary with medical terms and another
with Latin names of birds.

 NOTE

Word ships with an empty dictionary called Custom
Dictionary. Until you create other custom dictionaries,
all words that you add will be appended to this one.

 PROCEDURE

To create a custom dictionary, follow these steps:

1. Choose Tools ➤ Preferences and click on the Spelling icon or click on Options in the Spelling dialog
box to reach the Spelling category of the Preferences dialog box.

2. Click New.

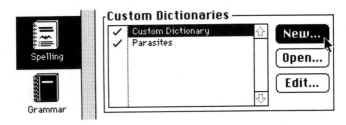

A Save dialog box will appear.

3. Give your new dictionary a name and click Save.

4. Close the Preferences dialog box.

PROCEDURE

To add a word to a custom dictionary during a spell check, click the Add Words To drop-down list and choose the appropriate dictionary. Don't forget to do this!

Then just click Add. The word will be appended to the selected dictionary.

 NOTE

You can review or delete words from a custom dictionary, in the Preferences dialog box. Choose Tools ➤ Preferences, click the Spelling icon, highlight the dictionary you want to amend, and click Edit. In the dialog box that appears,

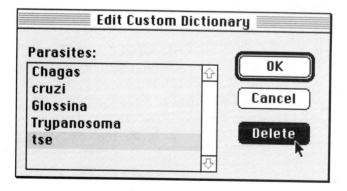

CUSTOMIZING

select and delete words you wish to remove from the dictionary. Click OK when you're done.

SEE ALSO

Part V, Spell Checking

Grammar

To reach the Grammar category, simply scroll until the Grammar icon is in view

Grammar

and click on it. The Grammar category will appear, as shown in Figure VII.6.

This category is complicated. Generally speaking, these are the functions you can control:

In **Rule Groups,** you can instruct word to apply or ignore certain rules of style or grammar. See the section *Rule Groups* below.

The **Catch** box lets you specify how conservatively Word should regard three specific grammar bugaboos: split infinitives, noun strings, and multiple prepositional phrases. To change a setting, click on the arrow to show the drop-down menu.

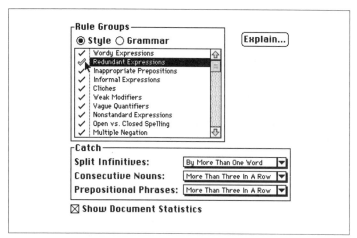

Figure VII.6: The Grammar category

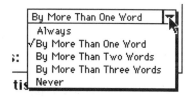

Then specify how fastidious you want Word to be.

Show Document Statistics instructs Word to display, at the end of every grammar check, a dialog box gauging the *reading difficulty level* of the document (see Figure VII.7). These figures are the result of Word's attempt to quantify your writing based upon certain abstruse formulas and equations.

```
░░░░░░░░░░ Document Statistics ░░░░░░░░░░
Counts:
   Words               2338         ┌──────────┐
   Characters         14174         │    OK    │
   Paragraphs           174         └──────────┘
   Sentences            137
Averages:
   Sentences per Paragraph     0
   Words per Sentence         17
   Characters per Word         4
Readability:
   Passive Sentences          9%
   Flesch Reading Ease      61.9
   Flesch Grade Level        8.8
   Flesch-Kincaid            7.8
   Gunning Fog Index         9.7
```

Figure VII.7: The Document Statistics dialog box

Rule Groups

Microsoft, in designing Word's grammar feature, under-
stood that not all writers will want to use strict style and
grammar rules. The Rule Groups box in the Grammar
category lets you specify which rules you want followed
and which ignored.

 PROCEDURE

**To specify which style or grammar rules Word should
use,** follow these steps:

1. In the Grammar category of the Preferences
   dialog box, click on either Style or Grammar. Each

presents a different list of rules in the scroll box below.

2. Click in the left-hand bar to enable or disable specific rules, as shown back in Figure VII.6. If you aren't sure what a rule means, highlight it and click Explain to see an explanation.

3. Close the Preferences dialog box. Any rules you have disabled will be ignored in all future grammar checks.

SEE ALSO

Part V, Grammar Checking

Thesaurus and Hyphenation

The Thesaurus and Hyphenation categories are simple and practically identical. To reach either the Thesaurus or Hyphenation category, simply scroll until the Thesaurus icon

Thesaurus

CUSTOMIZING

or the Hyphenation icon

Hyphenation

is in view and click on it. The desired category will appear, as shown in Figure VII.8. These categories look exactly alike.

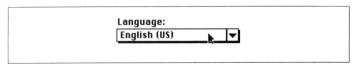

Language:

English (US)

Figure VII.8: The Thesaurus or Hyphenation category

You won't have many choices in the Language drop-down menu unless you've purchased additional foreign-language thesauri or hyphenation dictionaries from Microsoft or third parties.

TAKING COMMAND ▲

You can designate keyboard shortcuts for any command in Word. Furthermore, you can place any command on a menu, to make it easily accessible. Because there are practical limitations to the number of mnemonic keyboard combinations, you will probably find it most useful to assign shortcuts to commands you use very frequently, placing less-common commands on menus.

Adding and Removing Menu Commands

Word's default menu layout is quite logical, but all people work differently. You might even find that alternative configurations are useful for different tasks.

 PROCEDURE

To add or remove menu commands, follow these steps:

1. Choose Tools ➤ Commands. The Commands dialog box will appear, as shown in Figure VII.9.

2. As you can see, there is a lot going on in this box. To configure menus, scroll through the commands list until you find the command you want to add to or remove from a menu. You can scroll using the scroll bar or by typing the first letter of the command.

3. When you find the command, highlight it, as shown in Figure VII.9. An explanation of what the command does will appear in the Description box.

4. If the command is already on a menu, you can click Remove to delete it. If it is not on a menu, click Add to append the command to its default menu. You can add a command to a menu other than the default by clicking to reach the Menu drop-down list.

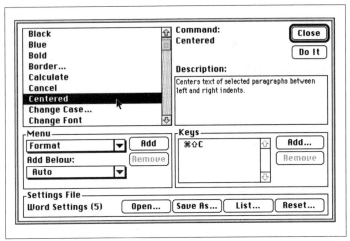

Figure VII.9: The Commands dialog box

Then choose the menu you want to add the command to. You can also specify where on the menu the command should go by choosing a position from the Add Below drop-down list.

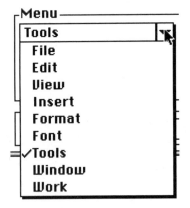

5. When you are finished, click Close.

 NOTE

You can add *separators,* the lines that appear on menus in between commands, wherever you like. Simply choose --Separator-- in the commands list and add it where you like.

 KEYBOARD SHORTCUT

The shortcut for removing a menu command is pressing ⌘-Option-– (the pointer will turn into a large minus sign) and choosing the command. The menu bar will flash to let you know that the command has been terminated.

Creating or Changing Keyboard Shortcuts

Word's keyboard shortcuts are well conceived, particularly if you don't have an extended keyboard. If you *do* have a keyboard with function keys, though, you might wish to replace the default assignments with other common commands. Simply by reassigning the keys F5 through F15, you can more than double the number of basic commands that are just a key or two away.

CUSTOMIZING

Also, some of Word's standard shortcuts are not all that easy to remember (⌘-Shift-Option-C for Tools ➤ Commands, for example). In these cases, you might want to add simpler shortcuts.

 PROCEDURE

To create or change keyboard shortcuts, follow these steps:

1. Choose Tools ➤ Commands to reach the Commands dialog box.

2. Scroll to find the desired command and highlight it.

3. If it already has a shortcut, it will appear in the Keys box. To delete a shortcut, highlight it and click Remove. If the command doesn't have a shortcut, click Add to create one. You will be asked to demonstrate the shortcut. Just press the keys you want in the combination. If the shortcut you choose is already assigned to another command, you will be given an opportunity to either abort the change or to reassign the shortcut.

It is usually *not* a good idea to replace standard commands such as Save (⌘-S), Print (⌘-P), or Open (⌘-O), because this can confuse other people who use your computer.

4. When you are finished, consider saving your configuration to a new settings file, as described in the section *Saving and Recalling Custom Configurations*. You might also wish to add the command and its shortcut to a menu.

5. To put your settings into effect, click Close.

KEYBOARD SHORTCUT

The keyboard shortcut to reach the Commands dialog box is ⌘-**Shift-Option-C**. The shortcut to assign a key combination is ⌘-**Shift-Option-←**. Press these keys and the pointer will turn into a bold command symbol (⌘). Then choose the command you want to assign a shortcut to and demonstrate the shortcut.

Saving and Recalling Custom Configurations

After you spend a long, gruelling afternoon getting your configuration just the way you want it, it's a good idea to save your settings under a new name. That way, if someone accidentally resets Word's configuration to the factory settings, you won't feel inclined to commit justifiable homicide.

 PROCEDURE

To save a custom configuration, follow these steps:

1. Make all the changes necessary to get your configuration just right.

2. Choose Tools ➤ Commands to reach the Commands dialog box if you're not in it already.

4. Click Save As in the Settings File options box.

A Save As dialog box will appear.

3. Give your settings file a relevant name, such as *Charlie's Settings,* and click Save.

 PROCEDURE

To recall a custom settings file, choose Tools ➤ Commands and click Open. An open dialog box will appear, listing all the settings files available. Double-click the one you want to use and click Close in the Commands dialog box. Word will replace the current configuration with the one in the custom settings file.

SNAPGUIDE TO FUTURE CUSTOMIZATION ▲

Most Macintosh programs—including Word—used to be single applications. Now, however, you see more and more Mac applications with enhancement products called *add-ons*. Add-ons are additional software that you can purchase to complement the main piece of software. QuarkXPress, for example, has add-ons called *Xtensions* that expedite four-color separations, prepress layouts, tables, and so on.

There are many advantages to this modular approach: for example, you need buy only those add-ons required for your work. Also, because add-ons free applications to perform their *basic* purpose (for example, a word processor can concern itself with just word processing, and not drawing), applications run faster and more efficiently. Thus, add-ons can take care of the "goodies" that we, perhaps misguidedly, have come to expect of programs.

In Word 5, there are already two utilities that are essentially separate from the application itself: Equation Editor and the drawing tool. The grammar and spell checkers, Find File, voice annotations, and the conversion files can be considered add-ons as well. New versions of Word will probably rely more and more on add-ons for specialized tasks. We'll almost certainly see some kind of macro add-on soon, and the next full upgrade of Word might include a chart utility and tool bar.

But why wait for these to come out? There are already many add-ons for Word 5. Let's look at a few.

Add-Ons from Alki

Many very useful add-ons are available from Alki Software Corporation, including a tool bar utility, an enhanced spell checker and thesaurus, and proofing tools for (at last count) 12 different languages.

The MasterWord Tools

The MasterWord CustomBar (shown in Figure VII.10) is a tool bar of icons that you can click to perform common functions. This saves you from having to remember keyboard shortcuts or select menu commands. The Custom-Bar adapts to your specific needs, too. Alki includes over 550 icons, which you can assign to any of 28 "slots."

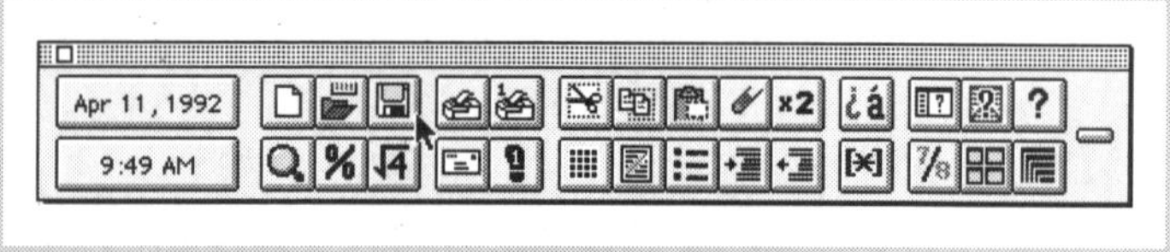

Figure VII.10: The MasterWord CustomBar

A great advantage of the CustomBar is that it can perform functions (with a single click!) that *don't even exist* as Word commands. For example, there are no "bulleted list," "print envelope," or "print watermark" commands in Word, yet there they are on the CustomBar, only a mouse-click away.

NOTE

▲ By default, the CustomBar appears above your document. My opinion, though, is that it is most useful to the left of documents, similar to the tool palettes found in drawing and desktop-publishing programs.

▲ In addition to the CustomBar, the MasterWord collection of tools includes Calc, a calculation utility; Seek, a file finder; and Scale, an application for calculating image-scaling ratios, as well as an enhanced help file and help index.

Comprehensive Spelling and Thesaurus

Two other potentially useful add-ons are the comprehensive spelling dictionary and thesaurus.

The comprehensive dictionary contains 74,100 more words than Word's standard dictionary (which has about 104,000), mostly medical and legal terms. Depending upon your purpose, this could eliminate the need for many of your custom dictionaries. If you add the speller, you will have a choice of which dictionary you want as your main dictionary, Word's standard—English (US)—or the comprehensive dictionary—English (US Legal & Medical).

Main Dictionary:

English (US)	▼

| English (US Legal & Medical) |
| √English (US) |

| Birds |
| Medical Terms |

The comprehensive thesaurus doubles the number of words you can look up with the Tools ➤ Thesaurus command and triples the number of synonyms.

NOTE

Alki's address is

> Alki Software Corporation
> 219 First Avenue N., Suite 410
> Seattle, WA 98109
> (800) 669-9673

QuickTime

Microsoft recently added to Word 5's arsenal of add-ons with the Microsoft Movie PIM (plug-in module). This utility allows you to insert QuickTime movies into your Word documents. *QuickTime* files are essentially little movies or clips of animation. You should strongly consider implementing them in your work, because readers will soon come to expect QuickTime to appear in all kinds of documents. In an online stockholder's report, for instance, you might see the president of a company giving a brief welcome to stockholders. In an online project proposal, you might see the project manager outlining a project's merits.

Movie PIM can play movies (including moving charts and graphs exported from Excel) when you double-click, insert movies from the menu, and even freeze frames or edit segments of movies. This add-on costs only $7.50.

INDEX

___

command buttons, 6

commands

adding to menus and keyboard shortcuts, 19–20, 246–251

repeating, 10, 63–64

selecting from menus with keyboard shortcuts, 8

selecting from menus with mouse, 7

undoing, 10, 63–64

Commands command, 19

copies, specifying number to print, 197

Copy command, 10, 60

cover pages, specifying for printing, 197

Create Publisher command, 11, 167

crosshair style mouse pointer, 44

current date, inserting in documents, 14

cursor

as dotted line, 62

positioning with the mouse, 32

CustomBar, 254–255

customizing

commands, 19–20, 246–251

dictionaries, 239–242

fonts, 236–237

general operations, 230–232

grammar checker, 242–245

menus, 234

open and save operations, 235–236

and saving changes, 251–252

screens, 232–233

spell checker dictionaries, 239–242

Thesaurus, 245–246

views and screens, 232–234

cut and paste operations, 10, 60–63

Cut command, 10, 60

D

daggers, specifying for footnotes, 132

data, clearing, 10

Date command, 14

DDE (dynamic data exchange), 168

Default Font command, 17

defaults. *See also* Preferences command

for fonts, 17, 236–237

for index placement, 160

G

⌘-G keyboard shortcut, 11, 221

glossaries
for automatic text features, 11
how to use, 111–113
importance of saving, 71

Glossary command, 11, 111–112

Go To command, 11, 220–221

grammar checker
as add-on utility, 253
advantages and disadvantages of, 75, 176
customizing, 242–245
starting, 18, 177

Grammar command, 18, 177–179

Graphics Smoothing printer effect, 206

gutter margins, 118

H

hanging indents, 31, 98–99
hard hyphens, 182–183
hard (manual) page breaks, 106

Header command, 13, 129, 218

headers, 13, 128–132, 218–219

header windows, opening, 13

Help command, 20, 69–70

hiding
nonprinting characters, 4, 12
ribbons, 12
rulers, 12
text, 81, 158, 199–201, 232

highlighting, text, 58–59

⌘-H keyboard shortcut, 11, 68

hyphenating, 18, 182–187, 193

Hyphenation command, 18

⌘-hyphen keyboard shortcut, 184

I

I-beam-style mouse pointer, 4

⌘-I keyboard shortcut, 16, 80

importing non-Word documents, 29

Normal command, 12, 41
normal view mode, 40–42
numbering
    lines or paragraphs, 19,
        101–103
    pages, 217–219

O

Object command, 15, 144
object linking
    embedding objects in
        documents, 169
    linking of documents,
        168–169
    publish and subscribe
        feature, 166–168
    System 7 feature with
        Word, 22–23, 166
objects, opening programs
    creating, 11
OK command button, 6
⌘-O keyboard shortcut, 8,
    27, 54
Open command, 8, 53
opening
    additional windows for
        documents, 20
    documents, 8, 27, 29–30
    drawing tool, 15

header and footer
    windows, 13
programs creating
    objects, 11
sections, 14
setting defaults for,
    235–236
support files, 27
⌘-Option-+ keyboard
    shortcut, 112
⌘-Option-– keyboard
    shortcut, 249
⌘-Option-hyphen key-
    board shortcut, 184
⌘-Option-I keyboard
    shortcut, 9, 118, 217
⌘-Option-N keyboard
    shortcut, 12, 42
⌘-Option-O keyboard
    shortcut, 12, 45
⌘-Option-P keyboard
    shortcut, 12, 48
⌘-Option-R keyboard
    shortcut, 12, 51
⌘-Option-Shift-hyphen key-
    board shortcut, 184
option boxes versus
    exclusive options, 7
Options command, 11
orientation, specifying for
    document pages, 9,
    203–205

frames, 45, 140
View menu, options on, 12–13
⌘-V keyboard shortcut, 10, 61, 189
Voice Annotation command, 14, 163–164
voice annotations, 163–165, 253
Voice Annotations command, 13, 164–165

W

Window menu, options on, 20
⌘-W keyboard shortcut, 8, 39
Word 5. *See also* System 7 with Word 5's features
customizing with Preference command, 19
quitting, 9, 71
starting, 26–27
Word Count command, 18, 188
word counts, obtaining, 18, 187–188
Word for Windows, saving Word documents for, 34

WordPerfect, saving Word documents for, 34
words. *See also* text
hyphenating, 18, 182–187
selecting with the mouse, 32
word wrap, 31
Work menu, when to use, 20
WYSIWYG style displays, 12

X

⌘-X keyboard shortcut, 10, 60
Xtensions add-on program, 253

Y

⌘-Y keyboard shortcut, 10, 64

Z

⌘-Z keyboard shortcut, 10, 64
zoom boxes, 3

Selections from The SYBEX Library

APPLE/MACINTOSH

Desktop Publishing with Microsoft Word on the Macintosh (Second Edition)
Tim Erickson
William Finzer
525pp. Ref. 601-4

The authors have woven a murder mystery through the text, using the sample publications as clues. Explanations of page layout, headings, fonts and styles, columnar text, and graphics are interwoven within the mystery theme of this exciting teaching method. For Version 4.0.

Encyclopedia Macintosh
Craig Danuloff
Deke McClelland
650pp. Ref. 628-6

Just what every Mac user needs—a complete reference to Macintosh concepts and tips on system software, hardware, applications, and troubleshooting. Instead of chapters, each section is presented in A-Z format with user-friendly icons leading the way.

Encyclopedia Macintosh Software Instant Reference
Craig Danuloff
Deke McClelland
243pp. Ref.753-3

Help yourself to complete keyboard shortcut charts, menu maps, and tip lists for all popular Macintosh applications. This handy reference guide is divided into functional software categories, including painting, drawing, page layout, spreadsheets, word processors, and more.

Introduction to Macintosh System 7
Marvin Bryan
250pp; Ref. 868-8

An engaging, plain-language introduction to the exciting new Macintosh system, for first-time users and upgraders. Step-by-step tutorials feature dozens of screen illustrations and helpful examples drawn from both business and personal computing. Covers the Desktop, working with programs, printing, customization, special accessories, and sharing information.

Mastering Adobe Illustrator
David A. Holzgang
330pp. Ref. 463-1

This text provides a complete introduction to Adobe Illustrator, bringing new sophistication to artists using computer-aided graphics and page design technology. Includes a look at PostScript, the page composition language used by Illustrator.

Mastering Microsoft Word on the Macintosh
Michael J. Young
447pp. Ref. 541-7

This comprehensive, step-by-step guide shows the reader through WORD's extensive capabilities, from basic editing to custom formats and desktop publishing. Keyboard and mouse instructions and practice exercises are included. For Release 4.0.

Mastering PageMaker 4 on the Macintosh
Greg Harvey
Shane Gearing
421pp. Ref.433-X

A complete introduction to desktop

publishing—from planning to printing—with emphasis on business projects. Explore the tools, concepts and techniques of page design, while learning to use PageMaker. Practical examples include newsletters, forms, books, manuals, logos, and more.

Mastering Ready, Set, Go!
David A. Kater
482pp. Ref. 536-0

This hands-on introduction to the popular desktop publishing package for the Macintosh allows readers to produce professional-looking reports, brochures, and flyers. Written for Version 4, this title has been endorsed by Letraset, the Ready, Set, Go! software publisher.

PageMaker 4.0 Macintosh Version Instant Reference
Louis Columbus
120pp. Ref. 788-6

Here's a concise, plain-language reference, offering fast access to details on all PageMaker 4.0 features and commands. Entries are organized by function—perfect for on-the-job use—and provide exact keystrokes, options, and cross-references, and instructions for all essential desktop publishing operations.

Up & Running with the Mac Classic
Tom Cuthbertson
160pp; Ref. 881-5

A fast, breezy introduction to computing with the Mac Classic. In just 20 steps, you get the fundamental information you need—without the details you don't. Each step takes only 15 minutes to an hour to complete, making this book a real timesaver.

Up & Running with Macintosh System 7
Craig Danuloff
140pp; Ref. 1000-2

Learn the new Mac System 7 in record time. This 20-step tutorial is perfect for computer-literate users who are new to System 7. Each concise step takes no more than 15 minutes to an hour to complete, and provides needed skills without unnecessary detail.

Up & Running with PageMaker on the Macintosh
Craig Danuloff
134pp. Ref. 695-2

Ideal for computer-literate users who need to learn PageMaker fast. In just twenty steps, readers learn to import text, format characters and paragraphs, create graphics, use style sheets, work with color, and more.

Up & Running with Norton Utilities on the Macintosh
Peter Dyson
146pp. Ref. 823-8

In just 20 lessons, you can be up and running with Norton Utilities for the Macintosh. You'll soon learn to retrieve accidentally erased files, reconstruct damaged files, find "lost files," unformat accidentally formatted disks, and make your system work faster.

Using the Macintosh Toolbox with C (Second Edition)
Fred A. Huxham
David Burnard
Jim Takatsuka
525pp. Ref. 572-7

Learn to program with the latest versions of Macintosh Toolbox using this clear and succinct introduction. This popular title has been revised and expanded to include dozens of new programming examples for windows, menus, controls, alert boxes, and disk I/O. Includes hierarchical file system, Lightspeed C, Resource files, and R Maker.

WORD PROCESSING

The ABC's of Microsoft Word (Third Edition)
Alan R. Neibauer
461pp. Ref. 604-9

This is for the novice WORD user who wants to begin producing documents in the shortest time possible. Each chapter has short, easy-to-follow lessons for both keyboard and mouse, including all the basic editing, formatting and printing functions. Version 5.0.

The Print Merge Helper Bar

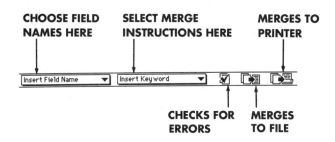

CHOOSE FIELD NAMES HERE

SELECT MERGE INSTRUCTIONS HERE

MERGES TO PRINTER

CHECKS FOR ERRORS

MERGES TO FILE

Equation Editor

RELATIONAL SYMBOLS

SPACES AND ELLIPSES

EMBELLISHMENTS

OPERATORS

ARROWS

LOGICAL SYMBOLS

SET THEORY SYMBOLS

MISCELLANEOUS SYMBOLS

GREEK CHARACTERS

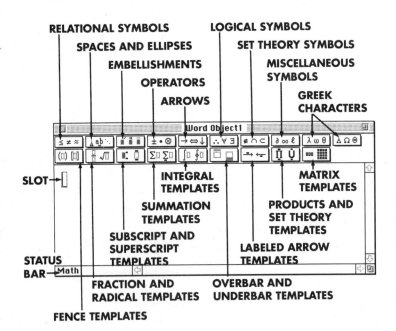

SLOT

STATUS BAR

INTEGRAL TEMPLATES

SUMMATION TEMPLATES

SUBSCRIPT AND SUPERSCRIPT TEMPLATES

FRACTION AND RADICAL TEMPLATES

FENCE TEMPLATES

MATRIX TEMPLATES

PRODUCTS AND SET THEORY TEMPLATES

LABELED ARROW TEMPLATES

OVERBAR AND UNDERBAR TEMPLATES